Mastering Data Analysis

A Step-by-Step Approach

Kiet Huynh

Table of Contents

Introduction

- About This Book

Welcome to "Mastering Data Analysis: A Step-by-Step Approach," a comprehensive guide crafted to empower readers with the skills and knowledge required to navigate the intricate landscape of data analysis. In this section, we will delve into the essence of this book, shedding light on its objectives, structure, and the unique value it brings to individuals seeking mastery in the realm of data analysis.

Understanding the Purpose:

At its core, this book is designed to be more than just a manual; it is a roadmap for individuals eager to harness the power of data and leverage it for informed decision-making. In an era where data is omnipresent, the ability to extract meaningful insights is a valuable skill. "Mastering Data Analysis" aims to bridge the gap between theoretical knowledge and practical application, providing a holistic approach that equips readers with the tools necessary to excel in the field.

Scope and Coverage:

The scope of this book is vast, encompassing a diverse range of topics within the realm of data analysis. From foundational concepts to advanced techniques, each chapter builds upon the previous, ensuring a gradual and structured learning experience. Whether you are a novice aiming to grasp the basics or an experienced practitioner seeking to refine your skills, the content is tailored to cater to various proficiency levels.

Key Features:

One distinctive feature of this book is its emphasis on a step-by-step approach. Each chapter unfolds systematically, presenting concepts in a logical sequence that facilitates comprehension and retention. Practical examples and real-world scenarios are woven throughout, illustrating how theoretical knowledge translates into actionable insights. Additionally, hands-on exercises and case studies are strategically integrated to reinforce learning and allow readers to apply newfound skills in a practical setting.

Interactive Learning:

Recognizing the importance of interactive learning, "Mastering Data Analysis" incorporates supplementary online resources. Readers can access datasets, code snippets, and additional exercises to enhance their understanding and refine their analytical capabilities. This interactive dimension transforms the learning process into a dynamic and engaging experience, fostering a deeper connection with the material.

Target Audience:

This book is crafted for a diverse audience, catering to the needs of students, professionals, and enthusiasts alike. Whether you are pursuing a career in data science, aiming to enhance your business analytics skills, or simply curious about the world of data, the content is structured to be accessible and relevant.

How to Navigate This Book:

To maximize the benefits of this guide, we provide guidance on how to navigate through its contents effectively. Whether you prefer a linear approach or wish to skip to specific topics, the user-friendly layout ensures a seamless reading experience. Additionally, each chapter concludes with a summary, highlighting key takeaways and setting the stage for the next section.

In essence, "Mastering Data Analysis: A Step-by-Step Approach" is not just a book; it is a companion on your journey to becoming a proficient data analyst. We invite you to embark on this learning adventure, where each page brings you closer to unraveling the secrets hidden within the vast expanse of data. Let the exploration begin!

- Who Can Benefit from This Guide

In the intricate world of data analysis, the potential beneficiaries of this comprehensive guide are as diverse as the data sets it seeks to unravel. "Mastering Data Analysis: A Step-by-Step Approach" is tailored to cater to a broad spectrum of individuals, each with unique aspirations, backgrounds, and levels of expertise. In this section, we will explore the various audiences who can derive significant value from the content of this guide.

1. Aspiring Data Analysts:

- This guide serves as an invaluable resource for individuals aspiring to embark on a career in data analysis. It provides a solid foundation, introducing fundamental concepts and gradually progressing to advanced techniques. Novices can leverage the step-by-step approach to build a robust skill set and gain confidence in handling diverse data sets.

2. Data Science Enthusiasts:

- Enthusiasts keen on exploring the dynamic field of data science will find this guide to be a compass guiding them through the intricacies of data analysis. Whether you are a student contemplating a future in data science or a professional looking to diversify your skill set, the content is curated to provide a holistic understanding of data analysis principles and methodologies.

3. Business Analysts and Decision Makers:

- Business analysts seeking to enhance their analytical prowess and decision-making skills will discover practical insights within these pages. The guide translates abstract concepts into tangible applications, empowering business professionals to extract meaningful information from data and make informed decisions that drive organizational success.

4. Students and Academia:

- Students pursuing degrees in fields such as statistics, computer science, or business will find this guide to be a valuable companion in their academic journey. It complements theoretical learning with real-world applications, bridging the gap between classroom knowledge and practical proficiency. Professors can also incorporate the book into their curricula to enrich the learning experience.

5. Professionals in Related Fields:

- Professionals in fields tangentially related to data analysis, such as marketing, finance, or healthcare, can leverage the guide to augment their analytical capabilities. The practical examples and case studies are designed to resonate with diverse industries, making the content applicable to a wide range of professional domains.

6. Self-Learners and Continuous Learners:

- Individuals driven by a thirst for knowledge and a commitment to continuous learning will find this guide to be a valuable asset. The step-by-step approach facilitates self-paced learning, allowing individuals to progress at their own speed. The interactive elements, such as hands-on exercises and online resources, cater to the self-learner's quest for practical application.

7. Data Professionals Seeking Skill Enhancement:

- Experienced data professionals, including data scientists and analysts, can use this guide to sharpen their skills and stay abreast of emerging trends in the field. The book delves into advanced topics, providing a refresher for seasoned practitioners and offering insights that contribute to professional growth.

8. Entrepreneurs and Start-Up Enthusiasts:

- Entrepreneurs navigating the complexities of running a business can benefit from the guide's emphasis on data-driven decision-making. Understanding how to extract valuable insights from data can be instrumental in shaping strategies, identifying market trends, and optimizing operations for startups and established businesses alike.

In conclusion, "Mastering Data Analysis: A Step-by-Step Approach" is not confined to a specific audience; rather, it opens its doors to a diverse community of learners and practitioners. Whether you are taking your first steps into the realm of data analysis or seeking to refine your expertise, this guide is crafted to be a versatile and invaluable companion on your journey toward mastering the art and science of data analysis.

- How to Use This Book

Welcome to the user guide for "Mastering Data Analysis: A Step-by-Step Approach." In this section, we will explore how to effectively navigate and utilize the content of this book to maximize your learning experience. Whether you are a novice embarking on your data analysis journey or an experienced professional looking to refine your skills, understanding how to use this book will be key to extracting the most value from its pages.

1. Sequential Learning Path:

- The book is structured in a logical sequence, with each chapter building upon the concepts introduced in the previous one. For those new to data analysis, we recommend following the chapters in order to ensure a solid foundational understanding. Each section is carefully crafted to introduce new concepts while reinforcing prior knowledge.

2. Interactive Elements:

- Throughout the book, you will encounter interactive elements designed to enhance your learning experience. Hands-on exercises, case studies, and real-world examples are strategically placed to reinforce theoretical concepts. Engage actively with these elements to apply the knowledge gained and solidify your understanding.

3. Online Resources:

- To complement your learning, this book provides access to online resources, including datasets and code snippets. These resources are intended to facilitate practical application, allowing you to work with real data and implement the techniques discussed in the book. Take advantage of these materials to reinforce your skills in a hands-on manner.

4. Practical Application:

- One of the primary goals of this book is to bridge the gap between theory and practice. Each chapter includes practical examples that demonstrate how to apply the concepts in real-world scenarios. As you progress, consider how the principles discussed can be adapted to your specific projects or professional context.

5. Summary and Key Takeaways:

- At the end of each chapter, you will find a summary highlighting key takeaways. Take the time to review these summaries, as they encapsulate the main points covered in the chapter. This will aid in reinforcing concepts and preparing you for the material in subsequent chapters.

6. Customized Learning Path:

- While a sequential approach is recommended, we understand that each reader's journey is unique. If you have prior experience in certain areas of data analysis, feel free to customize your learning path. The book is designed to accommodate readers at various proficiency levels, allowing you to focus on specific chapters or topics based on your needs.

7. Application to Real Projects:

- To derive maximum benefit from this guide, consider applying the acquired knowledge to your ongoing or future projects. Whether you are a student working on an academic assignment or a professional seeking to enhance workplace analytics, use the book as a practical tool to tackle real-world challenges.

8. Collaborative Learning:

- Encourage collaborative learning by discussing concepts with peers, participating in study groups, or seeking guidance from mentors. Sharing insights and exchanging perspectives can deepen your understanding and provide alternative viewpoints on the material.

9. Continuous Reference:

- This book is not meant to be read once and shelved. Treat it as a continuous reference guide. As you encounter new challenges or projects, revisit relevant chapters to refresh your memory and apply the knowledge in different contexts.

10. Feedback and Improvement:

- Your feedback is valuable in ensuring the continual improvement of this guide. If you have suggestions, questions, or insights, feel free to reach out to the author or publisher. Your input can contribute to the refinement of future editions and benefit the broader community of readers.

In conclusion, "Mastering Data Analysis: A Step-by-Step Approach" is designed to be a dynamic and practical resource for learners at various stages of their data analysis journey. By following these guidelines, you can unlock the full potential of the book, turning it into a personalized roadmap toward mastering the art and science of data analysis. Happy learning!

CHAPTER I
Getting Started with Data Analysis

1.1 Understanding the Role of a Data Analyst

1.1.1 The Importance of Data in Decision Making

In the dynamic landscape of today's information-driven world, the role of a data analyst has become pivotal in shaping the decision-making processes of organizations across various industries. In this section, we will delve into the profound significance of data and how it serves as the bedrock for informed decision-making, a responsibility at the core of a data analyst's role.

The Evolution of Data as a Strategic Asset:

As we navigate the digital age, data has transformed from being a mere byproduct of business operations to a strategic asset that organizations leverage for gaining competitive advantages. The recognition of data as a valuable resource has ushered in an era where decisions are increasingly data-driven. This paradigm shift underscores the vital role that data analysts play in extracting meaningful insights from the vast sea of information available.

Empowering Decision Makers:

At the heart of the data analyst's role is the empowerment of decision-makers. Organizations rely on data analysts to sift through large datasets, uncover patterns, and distill complex information into actionable insights. By translating raw data into comprehensible narratives, data analysts facilitate decision-makers in understanding trends, predicting outcomes, and devising strategies that align with organizational objectives.

Driving Informed Decision-Making:

In a business landscape characterized by uncertainty and rapid change, the ability to make informed decisions is a strategic advantage. Data analysts act as catalysts in this process, employing statistical models, algorithms, and analytical tools to interpret data. Through a meticulous examination of historical trends and current patterns, data analysts contribute to the creation of a decision-making framework grounded in empirical evidence.

The Interplay of Data and Business Strategy:

An effective data analyst not only comprehends the intricacies of data but also understands the broader business context. The alignment of data analysis with organizational goals is crucial. By recognizing patterns that impact revenue, customer satisfaction, or operational efficiency, data analysts become instrumental in steering the ship of business strategy towards success.

Enhancing Organizational Performance:

The insights derived from data analysis are not confined to influencing high-level strategic decisions; they permeate every facet of organizational performance. From optimizing marketing campaigns based on customer behavior to streamlining supply chain operations, data analysts contribute to efficiency gains and cost savings. Their work is a linchpin in creating a leaner, more agile, and responsive organizational structure.

Mitigating Risks through Predictive Analysis:

Understanding the past is valuable, but anticipating the future is transformative. Data analysts utilize predictive analysis techniques to forecast trends, identify potential risks, and recommend proactive measures. By integrating historical data with predictive modeling, organizations can preemptively address challenges, enhancing resilience in an ever-evolving business landscape.

Ethical Considerations in Data-Driven Decision Making:

As data assumes a central role in decision-making, ethical considerations become paramount. Data analysts must navigate the ethical dimensions of their work, ensuring the responsible use of data and safeguarding privacy. Awareness of the ethical implications of data analysis is integral to maintaining trust and credibility, both within the organization and among stakeholders.

Continuous Learning and Adaptability:

In a field marked by technological advancements and evolving methodologies, data analysts must exhibit a commitment to continuous learning. Staying abreast of emerging tools, techniques, and industry trends is essential. The ability to adapt to changing data landscapes ensures that data analysts remain effective contributors to organizational success.

In conclusion, the role of a data analyst is multifaceted, extending beyond the realms of numbers and algorithms. It is about harnessing the power of data to illuminate the path forward for decision-makers. The importance of data in decision-making cannot be overstated, and as organizations increasingly embrace a data-centric approach, the role of data analysts becomes increasingly vital in shaping a future where decisions are not just intuitive but also informed by the invaluable insights that data analysis provides.

To illustrate the significance of data in decision-making, let's delve into a few real-world examples that highlight the transformative impact of data analysis on organizations:

Example 1: Retail Analytics for Inventory Optimization

In the retail industry, data analysts play a crucial role in optimizing inventory levels. By analyzing historical sales data, a data analyst can identify patterns in customer buying behavior. For instance, during certain seasons or promotions, certain products may experience higher demand. By understanding these patterns, the retailer can optimize inventory, ensuring that popular items are well-stocked, reducing instances of stockouts, and minimizing excess inventory costs. This data-driven approach not only improves customer satisfaction by meeting demand but also enhances the overall efficiency of the supply chain.

Example 2: Financial Fraud Detection in Banking

Data analysts in the banking sector utilize advanced analytics to detect and prevent fraudulent activities. By analyzing transaction patterns, user behavior, and anomalies in real-time, data analysts can identify potentially fraudulent transactions. For instance, if a credit card is suddenly used for transactions in a location that is inconsistent with the user's historical behavior, it may trigger an alert for further investigation. This proactive approach to fraud detection not only protects customers but also safeguards the financial institution's reputation and financial integrity.

Example 3: Healthcare Predictive Analytics for Patient Outcomes

In healthcare, data analysts contribute to improving patient outcomes through predictive analytics. By analyzing historical patient data, including treatment outcomes, comorbidities, and demographic information, analysts can build models to predict the likelihood of certain medical conditions or complications. This enables healthcare providers to proactively identify high-risk patients, implement preventive measures, and personalize treatment plans. The result is not only improved patient care but also cost savings for both healthcare providers and patients.

Example 4: E-commerce Personalization for Customer Experience

E-commerce platforms leverage data analysis to enhance the customer experience through personalized recommendations. By analyzing user preferences, purchase history, and browsing behavior, data analysts can create algorithms that recommend products tailored to individual customers. This level of personalization not only increases the likelihood of customer satisfaction and repeat business but also contributes to the overall revenue of the e-commerce platform. It showcases how data-driven insights can be directly applied to enhance user engagement and drive business growth.

Example 5: Manufacturing Process Optimization

In manufacturing, data analysts contribute to process optimization by analyzing production data. By monitoring factors such as machine performance, defect rates, and production times, analysts can identify areas for improvement. For instance, by detecting patterns that precede machine failures, proactive maintenance schedules can be implemented, minimizing downtime and reducing maintenance costs. This application of data analysis in manufacturing illustrates how it leads to tangible improvements in operational efficiency and cost-effectiveness.

These examples underscore the varied and impactful ways in which data analysis influences decision-making across diverse industries. Whether it's optimizing inventory, preventing fraud, improving patient outcomes, personalizing customer experiences, or enhancing manufacturing processes, the role of data in decision-making is pivotal, and data analysts serve as the architects of this transformative process.

1.1.2 Key Responsibilities of a Data Analyst

In the dynamic landscape of data analysis, a data analyst assumes a multifaceted role that extends beyond the realm of number crunching and statistical modeling. This section explores the key responsibilities that define the core of a data analyst's role, emphasizing the diverse skill set and strategic contributions required in today's data-driven decision-making environment.

1. Data Collection and Acquisition:

- One of the primary responsibilities of a data analyst is to collect and acquire relevant data. This involves identifying potential data sources, collaborating with data engineers or administrators to access databases, and ensuring the quality and integrity of the data collected. The ability to navigate various data collection methods, whether through APIs, databases, or external sources, is crucial for a data analyst.

2. Data Cleaning and Preprocessing:

- Raw data is seldom ready for analysis. Data analysts are tasked with the responsibility of cleaning and preprocessing data to ensure accuracy and consistency. This involves handling missing values, addressing outliers, and transforming data into a format conducive to analysis. Proficiency in data cleaning techniques and tools is essential to extract meaningful insights.

3. Exploratory Data Analysis (EDA):

- Data analysts conduct exploratory data analysis to gain a preliminary understanding of the data. This involves creating visualizations, calculating summary statistics, and identifying patterns or trends. EDA is a critical phase in the analysis process, guiding subsequent analytical decisions and providing insights that inform the overall narrative of the data.

4. Statistical Analysis and Modeling:

- Leveraging statistical methods and modeling techniques, data analysts uncover patterns and relationships within the data. This may involve employing regression analysis, hypothesis testing, or machine learning algorithms, depending on the nature of the analysis. The goal is to extract actionable insights and make predictions that contribute to decision-making processes.

5. Interpreting and Communicating Results:

- A key responsibility is to translate complex analytical findings into understandable insights for non-technical stakeholders. Data analysts must possess effective communication skills to convey the implications of their analyses, whether through reports, presentations, or data visualizations. The ability to tell a compelling data-driven story is integral to ensuring that decision-makers can make informed choices.

6. Continuous Monitoring and Iterative Analysis:

- The data landscape is dynamic, and patterns may evolve over time. Data analysts are responsible for continuous monitoring of key metrics and iterating analyses as needed. This iterative process ensures that insights remain relevant and that organizations can adapt to changing conditions, thereby fostering a culture of continuous improvement.

7. Collaboration with Cross-Functional Teams:

- Collaboration is a cornerstone of a data analyst's role. Working closely with cross-functional teams, including business analysts, data engineers, and decision-makers, is essential. By understanding the broader context of business objectives, data analysts can align their analyses with organizational goals and contribute meaningfully to strategic initiatives.

8. Ethical Considerations and Data Governance:

- With great power comes great responsibility. Data analysts must adhere to ethical standards and considerations in their work. This involves ensuring data privacy, maintaining confidentiality, and navigating the ethical implications of their analyses. A commitment to data governance principles is integral to building and preserving trust within the organization.

9. Professional Development and Skill Enhancement:

- The field of data analysis is dynamic, with new tools and techniques continually emerging. Data analysts are responsible for investing in their professional development, staying abreast of industry trends, and enhancing their skill set. This commitment to continuous learning ensures that data analysts remain effective contributors in an ever-evolving landscape.

10. Strategic Decision Support:

- Ultimately, the role of a data analyst is to provide strategic decision support to the organization. By combining analytical rigor with a deep understanding of the business context, data analysts empower decision-makers to make informed choices that drive organizational success. This strategic advisory function cements the data analyst as a valuable asset in the decision-making hierarchy.

In summary, the key responsibilities of a data analyst encompass a spectrum of activities, from data acquisition and preprocessing to advanced statistical analysis and strategic decision support. The evolving nature of the field demands a versatile skill set, a commitment to ethical considerations, and effective communication abilities. As organizations increasingly recognize the pivotal role of data in shaping their future, data analysts stand at the forefront, wielding their expertise to illuminate the path forward through the vast sea of information.

1.2 Setting Up Your Data Environment

1.2.1 Choosing the Right Tools

In the realm of data analysis, the tools you choose to work with can significantly impact the efficiency, accuracy, and depth of your analyses. This section is dedicated to exploring the crucial decision of selecting the right tools for your data environment. From statistical software to programming languages, database systems to visualization tools, the choices you make at this stage lay the foundation for your entire data analysis journey.

1. Statistical Software:

- The choice of statistical software is fundamental to your data analysis endeavors. There are several prominent options in the market, each with its strengths and applications. Tools like R and Python, with libraries like Pandas and NumPy, are widely favored for their versatility and extensive statistical functionalities. On the other hand, proprietary software such as SPSS and SAS may be preferred in specific industries for their user-friendly interfaces and comprehensive statistical packages. Consider your specific needs, preferences, and the learning curve associated with each tool when making this decision.

2. Programming Languages:

- While statistical software provides a user-friendly interface, learning a programming language can significantly enhance your flexibility and control over analyses. Python and R are two of the most widely used programming languages in data analysis. Python's readability and extensive libraries, coupled with R's statistical prowess, make them popular choices. The decision between the two often depends on your prior programming experience, the tasks at hand, and the preferences of your data analysis team.

3. Database Systems:

- The selection of a database system is critical for efficient data storage and retrieval. SQL databases like MySQL and PostgreSQL are commonly used for structured data, offering robust relational database management systems. NoSQL databases like MongoDB excel in handling unstructured or semi-structured data, providing flexibility for large-scale, distributed systems. Consider the nature of your data, scalability requirements, and the compatibility of the database system with your chosen tools.

4. Data Cleaning and Preprocessing Tools:

- Data cleaning and preprocessing are integral steps in the data analysis pipeline. Tools like OpenRefine and Trifacta Wrangler facilitate the cleaning process by providing interactive interfaces for handling messy data. These tools automate tasks such as handling missing values, detecting outliers, and transforming data formats, streamlining the initial stages of analysis. Assess the scalability, ease of use, and compatibility of these tools with your chosen environment.

5. Visualization Tools:

- Communicating your findings effectively is as important as the analysis itself. Visualization tools like Tableau, Power BI, and Matplotlib in Python enable you to create compelling charts, graphs, and dashboards. The choice of visualization tool depends on your preferences, the complexity of your visualizations, and the need for interactivity. Ensure that the tool integrates seamlessly with your selected statistical software or programming language.

6. Collaboration Platforms:

- Collaboration is a key aspect of modern data analysis projects. Platforms like Jupyter Notebooks and Google Colab facilitate collaborative coding and documentation. These platforms allow multiple analysts to work on the same project simultaneously, fostering teamwork and knowledge sharing. Evaluate the collaborative features, version control options, and integration capabilities of these platforms to enhance the efficiency of your data environment.

7. Cloud Computing Services:

- Cloud computing has revolutionized data analysis by providing scalable and cost-effective infrastructure. Services like AWS, Azure, and Google Cloud offer a wide array of tools for data storage, processing, and analysis. Embracing cloud services can enhance the scalability and accessibility of your data environment, enabling you to handle large datasets and complex analyses seamlessly.

8. Machine Learning Frameworks:

- If your data analysis involves machine learning, choosing the right framework is paramount. TensorFlow and PyTorch are leading frameworks for deep learning, while scikit-learn is widely used for traditional machine learning tasks. Consider the complexity of your machine learning models, the ease of implementation, and the community support associated with each framework.

9. Documentation and Reporting Tools:

- Efficient documentation and reporting are essential aspects of a data analyst's workflow. Tools like Jupyter Notebooks, R Markdown, and LaTeX enable you to create well-documented analyses and reports. Choose tools that align with your preferred programming language and provide seamless integration with your chosen visualization and collaboration platforms.

10. Consideration of Cost and Resources:

- Lastly, consider the financial implications and resource requirements associated with your chosen tools. Open-source tools and languages often provide cost-effective solutions, while proprietary software may require licensing fees. Assess the availability of training resources, online communities, and documentation to ensure a smooth learning curve for you and your team.

In conclusion, the process of choosing the right tools for your data environment is a critical step in mastering data analysis. Carefully assess the requirements of your projects, the preferences of your team, and the scalability of the chosen tools. Remember that the tools you select will shape your analytical workflow and contribute to the success of your data analysis endeavors.

1.2.2 Configuring Your Workspace

Configuring your workspace is a crucial step in the journey of mastering data analysis. A well-organized and optimized workspace not only enhances your efficiency but also contributes to the overall quality of your analyses. In this section, we will explore the key considerations and best practices for configuring your workspace, ensuring that you are equipped with the optimal environment for effective data analysis.

1. Choosing the Right Hardware:

- The foundation of your data environment lies in the hardware you choose. The computing power of your machine significantly influences the speed and efficiency of your analyses. Consider the nature of your analyses, the size of your datasets, and the complexity of your computations when selecting or configuring your hardware. High-performance CPUs, sufficient RAM, and a fast storage solution are essential components for a smooth data analysis experience.

2. Operating System Selection:

- The choice of the operating system (OS) is a pivotal decision in configuring your workspace. Whether you opt for Windows, macOS, or a Linux distribution depends on your preferences, the compatibility of your chosen tools, and any specific requirements of your analysis tasks. Linux, in particular, is favored for its customization options, robust command-line interface, and widespread use in data science environments.

3. Development Environments:

- Selecting the right development environment is critical for a seamless data analysis workflow. Integrated Development Environments (IDEs) like Jupyter Notebooks, RStudio, or Visual Studio Code provide interactive and collaborative platforms for coding and analysis. Jupyter Notebooks, in particular, have gained popularity for their versatility, allowing you to intersperse code with explanatory text and visualizations.

4. Version Control Systems:

- Incorporating a version control system, such as Git, into your workspace is essential for tracking changes, collaborating with team members, and maintaining a record of your analysis history. Platforms like GitHub or GitLab offer remote repositories for hosting your projects, facilitating collaboration and providing a backup for your work.

5. Package Management:

- Efficient package management is crucial for handling libraries, dependencies, and extensions required for your analyses. Python relies on tools like pip and conda, while R uses CRAN. Ensure that your package management system is well-configured to install, update, and manage the libraries seamlessly. This helps maintain consistency across projects and reduces compatibility issues.

6. Setting Up Virtual Environments:

- Virtual environments allow you to create isolated spaces for different projects, preventing conflicts between dependencies. Tools like virtualenv for Python or renv for R enable you to create and manage these environments effortlessly. Virtual environments enhance reproducibility and ensure that your analyses can be replicated consistently.

7. Database Connection and Integration:

- If your analysis involves interacting with databases, configuring the connection and integration is paramount. Familiarize yourself with the appropriate drivers, connection strings, and authentication methods for your chosen database systems. This step ensures seamless data extraction, transformation, and loading (ETL) processes within your analysis workflow.

8. Customizing Text Editors and Shells:

- Text editors and shells are your primary interfaces for coding and running commands. Customize these tools to suit your preferences and enhance your productivity. Configure syntax highlighting, keyboard shortcuts, and themes to create a visually comfortable environment. Popular text editors include Sublime Text, Atom, and Vim, while shells like Bash or PowerShell offer powerful command-line interfaces.

9. Backup and Data Storage:

- Data security and backup strategies are integral components of configuring your workspace. Implement regular backup routines for your analysis projects, ensuring that critical data and code are safeguarded against unforeseen events. Explore cloud storage solutions or external drives to provide additional layers of redundancy.

10. Documentation and Note-Taking:

- Effective documentation is a hallmark of a well-configured workspace. Use tools like Markdown, Notion, or traditional notebooks to document your analyses, code explanations, and insights. Clear documentation not only aids in project management but also facilitates knowledge sharing within your team or community.

11. Security Considerations:

- Prioritize security in your workspace configuration. Implement encryption for sensitive data, use secure communication protocols, and stay informed about potential vulnerabilities in the tools and libraries you employ. Adhering to security best practices ensures the integrity and confidentiality of your analyses.

12. Continuous Learning and Optimization:

- The field of data analysis is dynamic, with new tools and techniques emerging regularly. Commit to continuous learning and optimization of your workspace. Stay updated on the latest developments, explore new tools, and refine your configuration based on evolving best practices.

In conclusion, configuring your workspace is a foundational step in the journey of mastering data analysis. By carefully considering hardware, operating systems, development environments, and security measures, you create an environment that empowers you to tackle complex analyses with efficiency and precision. Remember that your workspace is a dynamic entity, capable of evolving alongside the ever-changing landscape of data analysis tools and methodologies.

1.3 Introduction to Data Types

1.3.1 Numeric Data

In the expansive realm of data analysis, understanding the diverse nature of data types is foundational to extracting meaningful insights. Numeric data, a fundamental category, encompasses a wide range of information expressed in numerical form. This section delves into the intricacies of numeric data, exploring its significance, characteristics, and the analytical techniques employed in handling and interpreting such data.

1. Defining Numeric Data:

- Numeric data, at its core, consists of numerical values that represent quantitative information. These values can be integers or real numbers, capturing measurements, counts, or any data that can be expressed through numerical representation. In data analysis, numeric data is prevalent across various domains, providing a quantitative basis for statistical inference and analytical modeling.

2. Types of Numeric Data:

- Numeric data can be further categorized into discrete and continuous types. Discrete numeric data consists of distinct, separate values, often integers, representing countable items. Examples include the number of employees in a company or the quantity of products sold. On the other hand, continuous numeric data encompasses a range of values with infinite possibilities, typically measured with real numbers. Examples include temperature, height, or weight.

3. Measures of Central Tendency:

- Analyzing numeric data often involves determining its central tendency, which describes the central or average value in a dataset. Common measures include the mean, median, and mode. The mean, or average, is calculated by summing all values and dividing by the number of observations. The median represents the middle value when the data is sorted, and the mode is the most frequently occurring value.

4. Measures of Dispersion:

- Understanding the spread or dispersion of numeric data is essential for gaining insights into its variability. Measures such as the range, variance, and standard deviation provide insights into how much the values deviate from the central tendency. A larger range or standard deviation indicates greater variability within the dataset.

5. Histograms and Frequency Distributions:

- Visual representation is a powerful tool in numeric data analysis. Histograms, a graphical representation of the distribution of data, illustrate the frequency of values within predefined intervals or bins. Creating a frequency distribution, which tabulates the occurrences of specific values or ranges, offers a comprehensive view of the dataset's distribution.

6. Correlation and Regression Analysis:

- Numeric data analysis often involves exploring relationships between variables. Correlation measures the strength and direction of a linear relationship between two numeric variables. Regression analysis, on the other hand, models the relationship between a dependent variable and one or more independent variables. These techniques are fundamental in predictive modeling and understanding the interdependencies within numeric datasets.

7. Statistical Testing for Numeric Data:

- Numeric data analysis frequently involves statistical testing to make inferences about populations or draw conclusions from samples. T-tests, ANOVA, and regression analysis are common statistical tests applied to numeric data. These tests help assess the significance of observed differences or relationships, providing a robust foundation for decision-making.

8. Outlier Detection and Treatment:

- Outliers, extreme values that deviate significantly from the majority of data points, can impact the integrity of numeric data analysis. Detecting and addressing outliers is crucial for ensuring the accuracy and reliability of analytical results. Techniques such as box plots, Z-scores, or robust statistical methods aid in identifying and handling outliers appropriately.

9. Data Transformation and Normalization:

- Numeric data may require transformation to meet the assumptions of certain analytical methods. Logarithmic transformations, square root transformations, or standardization techniques are employed to normalize data distributions or address issues like skewness. These transformations enhance the validity of statistical analyses and model assumptions.

10. Time Series Analysis:

- Numeric data often evolves over time, leading to the realm of time series analysis. Time series data involves observations collected sequentially at regular intervals. Techniques such as moving averages, trend analysis, and seasonality decomposition are utilized to extract patterns, trends, and recurring cycles within time series datasets.

11. Machine Learning Applications:

- In the era of machine learning, numeric data forms the basis for developing predictive models and algorithms. Regression models, decision trees, neural networks, and other machine learning techniques thrive on numeric input features. Understanding the nuances of numeric data is pivotal for selecting, training, and evaluating machine learning models effectively.

12. Challenges and Considerations:

- Despite its ubiquity, numeric data analysis poses challenges, including issues of scale, skewness, and the impact of outliers. Data scientists and analysts must carefully consider these challenges and select appropriate techniques to address them, ensuring the robustness and reliability of their analyses.

13. Data Visualization for Numeric Data:

- Visualization plays a pivotal role in elucidating patterns and trends within numeric data. Scatter plots, line charts, and heatmaps are effective tools for portraying relationships, distributions, and variations. The visual representation of numeric data enhances comprehension and facilitates communication with stakeholders, aiding in the interpretation of complex analyses.

14. Geographic Mapping and Spatial Analysis:

- In certain contexts, numeric data is associated with geographic locations. Geographic Information System (GIS) tools enable the integration of numeric data with spatial information, allowing analysts to perform spatial analysis and visualize patterns across regions. Maps and spatial visualizations enrich the narrative of numeric data, particularly when exploring geographical variations and trends.

15. Ethical Considerations in Numeric Data Analysis:

- The responsible handling of numeric data includes a consideration of ethical principles. Data analysts must navigate issues related to privacy, bias, and fairness, especially when working with sensitive numeric information. Adherence to ethical guidelines ensures that analyses are conducted ethically and that the outcomes do not perpetuate inequalities or compromise individual privacy.

16. Emerging Trends in Numeric Data Analysis:

- The field of numeric data analysis is dynamic, with continuous advancements and emerging trends. Techniques such as explainable AI, automated machine learning, and federated learning are reshaping how numeric data is analyzed and utilized. Staying informed about these trends is essential for data analysts seeking to harness the latest tools and methodologies in their analytical endeavors.

17. Case Studies: Applying Numeric Data Analysis in Real-world Scenarios:

- To reinforce the concepts discussed, exploring real-world case studies provides practical insights into the application of numeric data analysis. Case studies might include scenarios from finance, healthcare, marketing, or other domains where numeric data is pivotal. Examining how numeric data analysis is implemented in diverse contexts enhances the reader's ability to apply these techniques in their own analytical projects.

18. Interactive Data Exploration:

- With the advent of interactive data exploration tools, analysts can now engage in dynamic, real-time exploration of numeric datasets. Platforms like Tableau, Plotly, or interactive Python libraries allow users to interact with visualizations, filter data, and uncover insights on the fly. Incorporating interactive elements into numeric data analysis enhances the exploration process and promotes a deeper understanding of the data.

19. Best Practices for Numeric Data Analysis:

- To optimize the accuracy and reliability of numeric data analysis, adherence to best practices is paramount. Documenting workflows, validating assumptions, and conducting sensitivity analyses are essential steps. Additionally, maintaining transparency in reporting methodologies and assumptions ensures the reproducibility of analyses and fosters a culture of data-driven decision-making.

20. Continuous Learning and Skill Enhancement:

- The landscape of numeric data analysis is ever-evolving, necessitating a commitment to continuous learning. Data analysts should invest in ongoing skill enhancement, staying abreast of new tools, methodologies, and emerging technologies. Engaging in online courses, participating in community forums, and attending industry conferences are avenues for staying informed and honing analytical skills.

Conclusion: Navigating the Numeric Landscape:

- Numeric data analysis, with its rich array of techniques and applications, stands as a cornerstone in the realm of data analytics. From foundational measures like central tendency to advanced machine learning models, the exploration of numeric data is a journey marked by challenges, discoveries, and the continual pursuit of insights. Armed with a comprehensive understanding of numeric data, data analysts embark on a transformative voyage, unraveling the complexities of datasets and contributing to informed decision-making across diverse domains. As the field evolves, the mastery of numeric data analysis becomes an enduring skill, empowering analysts to navigate the intricacies of the digital landscape and extract actionable knowledge from the numerical tapestry of data.

1.3.2 Categorical Data

In the expansive landscape of data analysis, categorical data emerges as a distinct and influential category that shapes the analytical journey. Understanding the nuances of categorical data is essential for data analysts seeking to glean insights from non-numeric information. This section delves into the intricacies of categorical data, exploring its definition, characteristics, and the methodologies employed in effectively handling and interpreting such data.

1. Definition and Characteristics of Categorical Data:

- Categorical data, also known as qualitative or nominal data, represents information that can be divided into distinct categories or groups. Unlike numeric data, which is measured on a scale, categorical data is non-numeric and often describes qualitative attributes. Examples include gender, colors, types of products, or educational qualifications. The fundamental characteristic of categorical data is that it places observations into distinct classes, allowing for the classification of entities based on shared characteristics.

2. Types of Categorical Data:

- Categorical data can be further classified into nominal and ordinal types. Nominal categorical data lacks a specific order or ranking among its categories. Examples include colors or types of fruits. On the other hand, ordinal categorical data possesses a meaningful order or hierarchy among its categories, albeit without a consistent interval. Examples include education levels or customer satisfaction ratings.

3. Representing Categorical Data:

- Effectively representing categorical data is crucial for analysis. One common method is through frequency tables, which tally the occurrences of each category in a dataset. Bar charts and pie charts are visual representations that offer a clear overview of the distribution of categorical data. These graphical representations aid in identifying patterns, trends, and outliers within different categories.

4. Measures of Central Tendency for Categorical Data:

- Unlike numeric data, which utilizes mean, median, and mode as measures of central tendency, categorical data relies on mode and proportions. The mode represents the most frequently occurring category, offering insights into the predominant attribute within the dataset. Proportions or percentages are often used to express the distribution of categories relative to the total number of observations.

5. Cross-Tabulation and Contingency Tables:

- Analyzing relationships between categorical variables involves techniques such as cross-tabulation and contingency tables. These methods organize data into a two-dimensional table, allowing analysts to observe how the frequency of one categorical variable is distributed across the categories of another. This facilitates the identification of associations, dependencies, or trends within the data.

6. Chi-Square Test for Independence:

- Statistical tests are essential tools for assessing the independence of categorical variables. The chi-square test for independence is a commonly used method to determine whether there is a significant association between two categorical variables. By comparing observed and expected frequencies, analysts can infer whether the variables are independent or if there is a meaningful relationship.

7. Handling Missing Data in Categorical Variables:

- Categorical data analysis necessitates addressing missing values within categories. Depending on the context, missing data may be treated by excluding observations, imputing values based on other variables, or employing advanced imputation methods. The approach chosen should align with the nature of the data and the potential impact on the analysis.

8. Feature Encoding in Machine Learning:

- In the context of machine learning, incorporating categorical data into predictive models requires feature encoding. This process involves converting categorical variables into a numerical format that machine learning algorithms can comprehend. Techniques like one-hot encoding or label encoding are commonly employed to represent categorical variables numerically, ensuring compatibility with machine learning algorithms.

9. Challenges and Considerations in Categorical Data Analysis:

- Categorical data analysis poses unique challenges, including the potential for sparsity, imbalances in category frequencies, and the risk of misinterpretation. Analysts must be cognizant of these challenges and implement appropriate strategies to mitigate biases and ensure the robustness of their categorical data analyses.

10. Real-World Applications of Categorical Data Analysis:

- The practical applications of categorical data analysis span diverse domains. From market segmentation and customer profiling to political polling and epidemiological studies, understanding and effectively analyzing categorical data are pivotal for making informed decisions. Real-world case studies showcase how categorical data analysis contributes to solving complex problems and informing strategic choices.

11. Interactive Data Exploration for Categorical Data:

- Interactive data exploration tools play a crucial role in unraveling insights from categorical data. Platforms like Tableau or Python libraries with interactive capabilities allow analysts to explore relationships, filter categories, and gain a deeper understanding of the patterns within categorical datasets. This interactivity enhances the exploration process and promotes a more comprehensive understanding of the data.

12. Ethical Considerations in Categorical Data Analysis:

- As with any data analysis, ethical considerations are paramount when dealing with categorical data. Ensuring privacy, avoiding biases in variable selection, and safeguarding against discriminatory practices are essential ethical considerations. Analysts must navigate these ethical nuances to uphold the integrity of their analyses and contribute to responsible and equitable decision-making.

13. Emerging Trends in Categorical Data Analysis:

- The landscape of categorical data analysis continues to evolve with emerging trends. Advancements in natural language processing (NLP) and sentiment analysis, coupled with the integration of categorical data into complex machine learning models, represent ongoing trends shaping the field. Staying informed about these developments positions analysts to harness the latest tools and methodologies in their categorical data analyses.

14. Conclusion: Navigating the Realm of Categorical Data:

- Categorical data, with its diversity and complexity, constitutes a pivotal component of the data analyst's toolkit. From understanding the fundamental types of categorical data to employing advanced statistical tests and machine learning techniques, analysts navigate a multifaceted landscape. Mastery of categorical data analysis empowers analysts to unravel patterns, draw meaningful insights, and contribute to informed decision-making across various domains. As the field continues to advance, the adept handling of categorical data stands as a foundational skill, enabling analysts to traverse the intricate pathways of qualitative information and derive actionable knowledge from diverse datasets.

To provide a practical understanding of categorical data analysis, let's explore examples that demonstrate the application of various techniques and methodologies.

Example 1: Market Segmentation in E-commerce

Consider an e-commerce dataset containing information about customer purchases, including categories such as product type, payment method, and geographic location. Categorical data analysis can be employed to segment the market based on customer preferences. Techniques like cross-tabulation and chi-square tests can reveal associations between product preferences and payment methods, enabling businesses to tailor marketing strategies for different customer segments.

Example 2: Political Polling and Voter Preferences

In political polling, categorical data is prevalent, capturing voter preferences for candidates, party affiliations, and policy priorities. Analyzing categorical data through methods like contingency tables allows political analysts to understand the relationships between different voter demographics and their preferences. Insights derived from categorical data analysis contribute to informed campaign strategies and policy messaging.

Example 3: Customer Feedback and Sentiment Analysis

For businesses collecting customer feedback through surveys or online reviews, categorical data analysis is instrumental in understanding sentiment. By categorizing feedback into positive, neutral, or negative sentiments, businesses can assess overall customer satisfaction. Textual data can be transformed into categorical variables, and sentiment analysis techniques can be applied to extract insights into customer sentiments, guiding improvements in products or services.

Example 4: Educational Assessment and Grade Distribution

In the context of education, categorical data analysis is applied to assess student performance. A dataset containing student grades, categorized by letter grades (A, B, C, etc.), can be analyzed using frequency tables and bar charts. This allows educators to understand the distribution of grades, identify areas for improvement, and tailor teaching strategies to address the needs of students with different performance levels.

Example 5: Healthcare Diagnosis and Disease Classification

In healthcare, categorical data analysis is integral to disease diagnosis and classification. Patient data, including symptoms, medical history, and diagnostic test results, can be categorized to identify patterns associated with specific diseases. Machine learning models trained on categorical data can aid in disease prediction and classification, assisting healthcare professionals in making accurate diagnoses and recommending appropriate treatments.

Example 6: Employee Satisfaction and Workplace Dynamics

For organizations conducting employee satisfaction surveys, categorical data analysis provides insights into workplace dynamics. Categorical variables, such as job satisfaction levels, can be analyzed to identify factors influencing employee morale. Cross-tabulation and chi-square tests can reveal correlations between satisfaction levels and variables like work-life balance, job role, or team dynamics, guiding HR strategies for improving workplace satisfaction.

These examples showcase the versatility of categorical data analysis across diverse domains. By effectively leveraging categorical data, businesses and organizations can make data-driven decisions, tailor strategies to specific demographics, and enhance their understanding of complex phenomena in various fields.

1.3.3 Time Series Data

In the dynamic landscape of data analysis, time series data stands as a distinctive and compelling category, offering a nuanced perspective on patterns, trends, and changes over time. Understanding the intricacies of time series data is essential for data analysts, as it opens the door to forecasting, trend analysis, and uncovering temporal dependencies within diverse datasets. This section delves into the multifaceted realm of time series data, exploring its definition, characteristics, and the methodologies employed in extracting meaningful insights.

1. Definition and Characteristics of Time Series Data:

- Time series data is characterized by a sequential arrangement of observations, each associated with a specific point in time. Unlike cross-sectional data, where observations are independent, time series data highlights the temporal aspect, revealing how a variable evolves over time. Common examples include stock prices, temperature records, sales figures, and physiological measurements. The fundamental characteristic of time series data lies in its inherent temporal order, enabling analysts to uncover patterns and trends that may be obscured in non-sequential datasets.

2. Components of Time Series Data:

- Time series data is often decomposed into various components, each contributing to the overall pattern. These components include trend, seasonality, cyclical variations, and irregular fluctuations. The trend represents the long-term movement or directionality of the data, while seasonality captures recurring patterns within specific time intervals. Cyclical variations reflect longer-term undulating patterns, and irregular fluctuations account for unpredictable deviations from the expected pattern.

3. Time Series Visualization Techniques:

- Visualizing time series data is a critical step in understanding its patterns and dynamics. Line charts, often employed to display temporal trends, provide a visual representation of how a variable changes over time. Additional techniques include candlestick charts for financial data, heatmaps for multivariate time series, and spectral analysis for exploring frequency components within the data. The choice of visualization method depends on the nature of the time series and the insights analysts seek to uncover.

4. Statistical Analysis of Time Series:

- Time series data analysis involves various statistical techniques to quantify and interpret patterns. Descriptive statistics, such as mean, median, and standard deviation, offer insights into the central tendency and variability over time. Autocorrelation and cross-correlation functions assess the correlation between observations at different time points, revealing temporal dependencies. Stationarity tests help ascertain whether the statistical properties of the time series remain constant over time.

5. Time Series Decomposition:

- Decomposing time series data into its constituent components facilitates a more granular analysis. Methods like moving averages, exponential smoothing, and Fourier analysis contribute to isolating trends, seasonality, and other components. By breaking down the time series, analysts gain a deeper understanding of the underlying factors driving the observed patterns.

6. Forecasting and Predictive Modeling:

- Time series data lends itself to forecasting and predictive modeling, where analysts leverage historical observations to predict future values. Techniques such as autoregressive integrated moving average (ARIMA) models, exponential smoothing methods, and machine learning algorithms like recurrent neural networks (RNNs) or Long Short-Term Memory (LSTM) networks are applied to project future trends. The accuracy of forecasts depends on the quality of the historical data and the appropriateness of the chosen model.

7. Seasonal Adjustment:

- Seasonal adjustment is a critical step in time series analysis, particularly when dealing with data exhibiting regular patterns at specific intervals. Removing seasonality enhances the clarity of underlying trends and enables a more accurate assessment of the impact of external factors. Analysts use techniques like differencing, ratio-to-moving-average adjustment, or applying seasonal decomposition of time series (STL) methods to achieve effective seasonal adjustment.

8. Anomaly Detection in Time Series:

- Identifying anomalies or outliers within time series data is crucial for detecting irregularities or unexpected events. Techniques such as Z-score analysis, machine learning models, or threshold-based methods aid in pinpointing deviations from the expected pattern. Anomaly detection is valuable in diverse domains, from fraud detection in financial transactions to monitoring equipment failures in industrial settings.

9. Time Series in Finance and Economics:

- Time series data plays a pivotal role in finance and economics, where analysts leverage historical price movements, economic indicators, and market trends to make informed predictions. Stock prices, exchange rates, GDP growth rates, and unemployment figures are examples of time series data extensively analyzed in these domains. The application of time series analysis contributes to risk assessment, investment strategies, and economic policy formulation.

10. Temporal Data in Healthcare:

- In healthcare, time series data is prevalent in monitoring patient vital signs, disease progression, and treatment outcomes. Electronic health records, wearable devices, and medical sensors generate vast amounts of temporal data. Time series analysis in healthcare facilitates early detection of anomalies, predictive modeling for patient outcomes, and optimizing treatment protocols based on temporal patterns.

11. Challenges and Considerations in Time Series Data Analysis:

- Time series data analysis presents unique challenges, including the need for handling missing data, addressing non-stationarity, and selecting appropriate forecasting models. The impact of external events, such as economic recessions or global pandemics, further complicates the analysis. Analysts must navigate these challenges with a nuanced understanding of the temporal intricacies inherent in time series data.

12. Integration of External Factors:

- Time series data analysis gains depth when integrated with external factors that may influence the observed patterns. This may include incorporating economic indicators, weather data, or social events to enhance the predictive capabilities of models. The integration of external factors acknowledges the interconnected nature of time series data with the broader context in which it operates.

13. Machine Learning Applications in Time Series Analysis:

- The intersection of machine learning and time series analysis opens avenues for advanced modeling and prediction. Machine learning algorithms, including support vector machines, random forests, and neural networks, enhance the accuracy of time series forecasts. Feature engineering, hyperparameter tuning, and model ensembling are techniques employed to optimize machine learning models for time series data.

14. Real-Time and Streaming Time Series Data:

- With the advent of real-time data streams from IoT devices, sensors, and online platforms, the analysis of streaming time series data has become increasingly relevant. Techniques like online learning algorithms, sliding window approaches, and adaptive forecasting models accommodate the continuous influx of data, enabling timely decision-making and response.

15. Ethical Considerations in Time Series Data Analysis:

- Ethical considerations in time series data analysis revolve around privacy, transparency, and the responsible use of predictive models. As temporal data often involves personal information and influences decision-making, analysts must adhere to ethical guidelines to ensure the fair and unbiased treatment of individuals represented in the data.

16. Emerging Trends in Time Series Analysis:

- Time series analysis continues to evolve with emerging trends such as explainable AI, interpretable machine learning models, and advancements in automated forecasting. The integration of interpretable models addresses the black-box nature of certain algorithms, providing transparency in the decision-making process. Staying abreast of these trends positions analysts to harness the latest tools and methodologies in time series analysis.

17. Conclusion: Navigating the Temporal Landscape:

- Time series data analysis, with its temporal intricacies and forecasting capabilities, stands as a cornerstone in the realm of data analytics. From visualizing temporal patterns to forecasting future trends, analysts navigate a diverse landscape marked by challenges and discoveries. Mastery of time series data empowers analysts to unlock valuable insights, make informed predictions, and contribute to strategic decision-making across various domains. As the field advances, the adept handling of temporal data remains an enduring skill, enabling analysts to traverse the intricacies of time and unveil the hidden narratives within sequential datasets.

To concretize the concepts discussed in the exploration of time series data, let's delve into real-world examples that highlight the application of various techniques and methodologies.

Example 1: Stock Price Analysis

Consider a dataset representing the daily closing prices of a publicly traded company's stock over several years. This time series data holds invaluable insights for investors and financial analysts. By visualizing the stock prices over time, analysts can identify trends, seasonality, and potential cyclical patterns. Time series forecasting models can be employed to predict future stock prices, aiding investors in making informed decisions about buying or selling stocks.

Example 2: Temperature Variation Over Seasons

Imagine a dataset recording daily temperatures in a city over the course of several years. This time series data exhibits both seasonality and trends. Through time series visualization, analysts can discern recurring temperature patterns corresponding to different seasons. Applying seasonal adjustment techniques allows for a clearer understanding of long-term temperature trends, aiding meteorologists in predicting future temperature variations and identifying climate change trends.

Example 3: Website Traffic and User Engagement

For online platforms, time series data is crucial for understanding user behavior and optimizing website performance. Consider a dataset tracking daily website traffic, user clicks, and engagement metrics over time. Time series analysis can unveil daily and weekly patterns in user activity, helping businesses identify peak hours and optimize their online presence. Forecasting models can predict future website traffic, allowing companies to allocate resources efficiently and enhance user experience.

Example 4: Disease Surveillance and Epidemic Prediction

In the healthcare domain, time series data plays a vital role in monitoring the spread of diseases. Imagine a dataset containing daily reported cases of a contagious disease. Time series analysis enables epidemiologists to identify patterns, detect anomalies, and forecast potential outbreaks. This data-driven approach aids in allocating healthcare resources, implementing preventive measures, and formulating effective public health strategies.

Example 5: Energy Consumption Patterns

Utilities and energy companies rely on time series data to understand and manage energy consumption patterns. A dataset capturing hourly or daily energy usage for a city or region reveals temporal dependencies influenced by factors like weather, time of day, and economic activities. Time series analysis helps in predicting peak energy demand, optimizing resource allocation, and planning for future energy infrastructure needs.

Example 6: Social Media Activity Metrics

For social media platforms, time series data is abundant, tracking metrics such as daily active users, post engagement, and trending topics. Analyzing these time series datasets helps social media companies understand user engagement patterns, identify popular content, and predict trends. Forecasting models can assist in anticipating user behavior and informing content creation strategies.

These examples illustrate the diverse applications of time series data analysis across different domains. Whether in finance, meteorology, healthcare, or digital platforms, the ability to uncover temporal patterns and forecast future trends empowers analysts to make informed decisions, optimize processes, and contribute to advancements in their respective fields.

CHAPTER II
Essential Data Analysis Techniques

2.1 Exploratory Data Analysis (EDA)

2.1.1 Visualizing Data with Charts and Graphs

Visualizing data is a fundamental aspect of the exploratory data analysis (EDA) process, providing a powerful means to unravel patterns, trends, and insights inherent in datasets. In this section, we delve into the various techniques and principles behind visualizing data using charts and graphs, exploring how different visualization tools enhance our understanding of complex datasets.

1. Importance of Data Visualization:

- Data visualization serves as a bridge between raw data and actionable insights. It transforms abstract numbers and statistics into visual representations that are easily interpretable. Effective visualization not only simplifies the communication of findings but also facilitates the identification of patterns, outliers, and relationships within the data. Whether working with small datasets or large, complex datasets, the ability to create meaningful visualizations is a cornerstone of proficient data analysis.

2. Types of Charts and Graphs:

- The choice of visualization depends on the nature of the data and the insights one aims to derive. Common types of charts and graphs include:

- **Bar Charts:** Suitable for comparing categories and displaying the distribution of categorical data.
- **Line Charts:** Ideal for showing trends over time or relationships between variables.
- **Scatter Plots:** Effective for visualizing the relationship between two continuous variables, highlighting correlations or patterns.
- **Histograms:** Useful for illustrating the distribution of a single variable and identifying underlying patterns.
- **Pie Charts:** Helpful for displaying the proportional contributions of different categories to a whole.
- **Box Plots (Box-and-Whisker Plots):** Valuable for visualizing the distribution and variability of a dataset, including outliers.
- **Heatmaps:** Effective for representing the magnitude of a phenomenon across two categorical variables, often used in correlation matrices.

Each type of chart serves a specific purpose, and the judicious selection of visualization tools enhances the clarity and effectiveness of data communication.

3. Principles of Effective Data Visualization:

- Creating impactful visualizations involves adhering to certain principles:

- **Simplicity:** Keep visualizations clear and concise to convey information efficiently.
- **Relevance:** Ensure that the chosen visualization method aligns with the nature of the data and the insights sought.
- **Accuracy:** Accurately represent data to avoid misinterpretation and misinformation.

- **Consistency:** Maintain consistency in labeling, color usage, and scale to enhance viewer comprehension.

- **Interactivity:** Incorporate interactive elements when applicable to engage users and enable deeper exploration of the data.

Following these principles contributes to the creation of visualizations that resonate with the audience and effectively communicate the story behind the data.

4. Bar Charts and Their Applications:

- Bar charts are versatile visualizations suitable for various scenarios:

- **Comparing Categories:** Bar charts excel at comparing the magnitude of different categories. For instance, in a sales dataset, a bar chart can showcase the sales performance of different products.

- **Distribution of Categorical Data:** When dealing with categorical data, a bar chart helps visualize the frequency or count of each category.

- **Time Series Analysis:** In time series data, bar charts can represent the distribution of values at specific time points, providing a snapshot of trends over time.

- **Comparison Across Subgroups:** Bar charts are effective for comparing subgroups within a category, such as sales performance across different regions or departments.

5. Line Charts for Trend Analysis:

- Line charts are instrumental in visualizing trends and relationships:

- **Time Series Trends:** When exploring data over time, line charts help identify patterns, seasonality, and overall trends.

- **Correlation Between Variables:** Line charts can reveal correlations between two continuous variables, helping identify relationships and dependencies.

- **Comparing Multiple Series:** Line charts facilitate the comparison of multiple series on a single plot, aiding in the assessment of relative performance.

6. Scatter Plots for Relationship Exploration:

- Scatter plots are essential for understanding relationships between two continuous variables:

- **Correlation Assessment:** Scatter plots provide a visual representation of the correlation between two variables, revealing patterns such as positive, negative, or no correlation.

- **Identification of Outliers:** Outliers, anomalies, or unusual patterns in data become apparent in scatter plots, aiding in anomaly detection and further investigation.

7. Practical Application of Heatmaps:

- Heatmaps offer a visually compelling way to represent the magnitude of a phenomenon across two categorical variables:

- **Correlation Matrices:** In complex datasets with multiple variables, a heatmap of the correlation matrix provides a concise overview of inter-variable relationships.

- **Spatial Analysis:** Heatmaps are valuable in spatial analysis, representing data variations across geographical regions or within a spatial context.

8. Interactive Visualization Tools:

- The integration of interactive elements in visualizations enhances user engagement and facilitates deeper exploration. Tools such as Tableau, Power BI, and Python libraries like Plotly enable the creation of interactive dashboards, allowing users to interact with the data dynamically.

9. Case Studies: Real-World Application of Data Visualization:

- The section concludes with case studies showcasing real-world applications of data visualization in diverse domains, including business analytics, scientific research, and social sciences. These case studies illustrate how effective visualization contributes to informed decision-making and enhances the understanding of complex datasets.

10. Future Trends in Data Visualization:

- The landscape of data visualization continues to evolve with emerging trends, including augmented reality (AR) visualizations, immersive storytelling techniques, and advancements in 3D visualization. Staying abreast of these trends equips data analysts with the tools and methodologies to create innovative and impactful visualizations.

11. Conclusion: Harnessing the Power of Visual Storytelling:

- Mastering the art of visualizing data is akin to becoming a storyteller, where each chart or graph narrates a part of the data's story. In this section, we have explored the principles, types, and applications of data visualization techniques, emphasizing their role in transforming raw data into meaningful insights. As data analysts embark on the journey of exploratory data analysis, the ability to wield visualizations effectively becomes a potent tool for unraveling the intricate narratives hidden within datasets.

2.1.2 Descriptive Statistics

Descriptive statistics form a cornerstone of exploratory data analysis (EDA), providing a comprehensive and concise summary of key features within a dataset. This section delves into the realm of descriptive statistics, exploring the various measures and techniques used to characterize the central tendency, variability, and distribution of data.

1. Introduction to Descriptive Statistics:

- Descriptive statistics aim to distill complex datasets into meaningful and interpretable summaries. These statistical measures offer insights into the overall structure of the data, allowing analysts to grasp its fundamental characteristics. Key aspects of descriptive statistics include measures of central tendency, measures of variability, and the shape of the data distribution.

2. Measures of Central Tendency:

- *Mean:* The arithmetic mean, or average, is a central measure that represents the sum of all data points divided by the total number of observations. While widely used, the mean is sensitive to outliers and extreme values.

- *Median:* The median is the middle value when data is arranged in ascending or descending order. It is less affected by outliers and provides a robust measure of central tendency.

- *Mode:* The mode represents the most frequently occurring value in a dataset. In cases where there are multiple modes, the data is considered multimodal.

- Each measure of central tendency offers unique insights into the center of the data distribution, catering to different scenarios and data characteristics.

3. Measures of Variability:

- *Range:* The range is the difference between the maximum and minimum values in a dataset, providing a simple but limited measure of variability.

- *Variance:* Variance quantifies the dispersion of data points around the mean. It is calculated by averaging the squared differences between each data point and the mean.

- *Standard Deviation:* The standard deviation is the square root of the variance, offering a more interpretable measure of variability. It indicates the average deviation of data points from the mean.

- *Interquartile Range (IQR):* IQR measures the range within which the middle 50% of data values lie. It is less influenced by extreme values and provides a robust measure of variability.

- Understanding variability is crucial for assessing the spread and consistency of data, aiding in the identification of potential outliers or clusters.

4. Skewness and Kurtosis:

- *Skewness:* Skewness measures the asymmetry of a distribution. Positive skewness indicates a tail to the right, while negative skewness suggests a tail to the left. Skewness helps analysts understand the departure of data from a symmetric distribution.

- *Kurtosis:* Kurtosis assesses the "tailedness" of a distribution. High kurtosis indicates heavy tails, while low kurtosis suggests light tails. Kurtosis provides insights into the concentration of data around the mean.

- Skewness and kurtosis contribute to a more nuanced understanding of the shape and characteristics of a distribution beyond central tendency and variability.

5. Frequency Distributions:

- Constructing frequency distributions involves grouping data into intervals or bins and counting the number of observations within each interval. Histograms, bar charts, and frequency polygons are visual representations of frequency distributions, providing insights into the density and patterns within the data.

6. Practical Applications of Descriptive Statistics:

- *Business Analytics:* Descriptive statistics are instrumental in business analytics for summarizing performance metrics, assessing customer behavior, and guiding strategic decision-making.

- *Healthcare:* In healthcare, descriptive statistics aid in summarizing patient data, assessing the effectiveness of treatments, and identifying trends in health outcomes.

- *Social Sciences:* Descriptive statistics are widely used in social sciences for summarizing survey data, analyzing demographic trends, and understanding social phenomena.

- *Quality Control:* Industries employ descriptive statistics for quality control, monitoring production processes, and ensuring consistency in product performance.

7. Limitations and Considerations:

- While descriptive statistics offer valuable insights, it is essential to acknowledge their limitations. They provide a summary of existing data but do not establish causation or inferential relationships. Additionally, outliers can significantly impact certain measures, necessitating caution in their interpretation.

8. Reporting Descriptive Statistics:

- Communicating descriptive statistics effectively involves clear and concise reporting. Tables, charts, and visualizations enhance the presentation of key measures, making it accessible to both technical and non-technical audiences.

9. Advanced Descriptive Techniques:

- Beyond basic measures, advanced techniques such as quartile deviation, geometric mean, and harmonic mean offer additional perspectives on data characteristics. These measures cater to specific scenarios and data distributions.

10. Conclusion: Unveiling Patterns in the Data Tapestry:

- Descriptive statistics, as the weaver of the data narrative, unravel patterns, trends, and characteristics embedded within datasets. This section has navigated the landscape of central tendency, variability, and distribution shape, equipping data analysts with tools to decipher the intricate tapestry of information. As analysts embark on the journey of exploratory data analysis, the adept use of descriptive statistics illuminates the path toward deeper insights and informed decision-making.

2.2 Data Cleaning and Preprocessing

2.2.1 Handling Missing Data

Handling missing data is a crucial step in the data cleaning and preprocessing phase of the analytical journey. In this section, we delve into the challenges posed by missing data, explore various strategies for imputation, and discuss best practices for ensuring data integrity and analytical robustness.

1. Understanding the Impact of Missing Data:

- Missing data is a pervasive issue in datasets and can significantly impact the quality and reliability of analyses. It can lead to biased results, reduced statistical power, and misinterpretation of findings. Before deciding on a specific imputation strategy, it is essential to assess the nature and patterns of missingness within the dataset.

2. Types of Missing Data:

- *Missing Completely at Random (MCAR):* The occurrence of missing data is entirely random and unrelated to any observed or unobserved variables. This type of missingness is considered less problematic for analyses.

- *Missing at Random (MAR):* The probability of missing data depends on observed variables but not on the missing values themselves. MAR is a common scenario in observational studies.

- *Missing Not at Random (MNAR):* The missingness is related to unobserved variables, making it challenging to address. MNAR introduces potential biases and requires careful consideration during imputation.

3. Imputation Techniques:

- *Mean/Median Imputation:* Replace missing values with the mean or median of the observed values for that variable. This method is simple but may not be suitable for variables with skewed distributions.

- *Linear Regression Imputation:* Use regression models to predict missing values based on other observed variables. This method assumes a linear relationship between variables and may be sensitive to outliers.

- *Multiple Imputation:* Generate multiple imputed datasets, each reflecting the uncertainty associated with missing values. Analyze these datasets separately and pool the results for more robust conclusions.

- *K-Nearest Neighbors (KNN) Imputation:* Impute missing values based on the values of their k-nearest neighbors in the observed data. This method is effective when there is a meaningful distance metric between observations.

- *Interpolation and Extrapolation:* For time-series data, missing values can be imputed using interpolation (estimating values within observed data points) or extrapolation (estimating values beyond observed data points).

4. Best Practices for Handling Missing Data:

- *Understand the Missing Data Mechanism:* Determine whether missing data is MCAR, MAR, or MNAR, as this understanding guides the selection of appropriate imputation methods.

- *Evaluate Imputation Impact:* Assess the impact of imputation on the distribution of variables, correlations, and statistical measures. Imputed values should preserve the original characteristics of the data as much as possible.

- *Consider Multiple Imputation:* When feasible, opt for multiple imputation to account for uncertainty in imputed values and obtain more reliable and robust results.

- *Document Imputation Processes:* Clearly document the chosen imputation strategy, reasons for selecting it, and any assumptions made during the imputation process. Transparency in imputation methods enhances the reproducibility of analyses.

5. Dealing with Outliers During Imputation:

- Outliers can significantly influence imputation outcomes. It's essential to address outliers before or during the imputation process to prevent their undue influence on imputed values.

6. Practical Applications and Case Studies:

- Explore real-world examples where handling missing data played a pivotal role in the success of analytical endeavors. Case studies illustrate the challenges faced, the chosen imputation strategies, and the impact on analytical outcomes.

7. Tools and Software for Missing Data Handling:

- Review popular tools and software packages that facilitate efficient handling of missing data, including Python libraries like Pandas and Scikit-learn, and R packages like mice and Amelia.

8. Ethical Considerations in Handling Missing Data:

- Discuss ethical considerations related to imputation, emphasizing transparency, the potential impact on research outcomes, and the responsibility of analysts to communicate the limitations introduced by imputed data.

9. Future Trends in Missing Data Handling:

- Explore emerging trends and methodologies in the field of missing data handling, including advancements in machine learning techniques for imputation and the integration of domain knowledge into imputation models.

10. Conclusion: Navigating the Missing Data Maze:

- The effective handling of missing data is a critical skill for data analysts and researchers. This section has provided a comprehensive overview of the challenges posed by missing data, strategies for imputation, and best practices for maintaining data integrity. As data scientists navigate the intricate landscape of missing data, they are equipped with a toolkit of methodologies and considerations to ensure the reliability and validity of their analyses.

Example Scenario: Handling Missing Data in a Clinical Study

Imagine you are a data analyst tasked with analyzing a clinical dataset focused on evaluating the effectiveness of a new drug in treating a specific medical condition. The dataset includes information on patient demographics, medical history, treatment details, and various health metrics measured at multiple time points.

1. Identifying Missing Data:

Upon initial examination, you discover that some patients have missing values for key variables, such as baseline health measurements and certain demographic information. The missingness seems non-random, as patients with more severe conditions appear to have more missing data.

2. Understanding the Missing Data Mechanism:

Your first step is to understand the missing data mechanism. Through discussions with the study team, you learn that some patients missed scheduled follow-up appointments due to the severity of their condition or other personal reasons. This suggests a Missing Not at Random (MNAR) mechanism.

3. Imputation Strategy:

Given the MNAR nature of the missing data, you decide to employ a combination of techniques. For variables where missingness is related to the severity of the condition, you opt for multiple imputation using predictive models that consider observed health metrics and medical history. For variables where missingness is more random, you choose mean imputation.

4. Evaluating Imputation Impact:

After imputation, you carefully assess the impact on the distribution of key variables and correlations between variables. You compare statistical measures and visualizations of the original and imputed datasets to ensure that imputation does not introduce biases or distort the overall patterns in the data.

5. Addressing Outliers:

You notice outliers in some health metrics and decide to address them before imputation. Outliers are handled using robust statistical methods to prevent them from unduly influencing the imputation process.

6. Ethical Considerations:

You document the imputation process transparently, highlighting the chosen strategies and acknowledging the potential limitations introduced by imputed data. Ethical considerations are paramount, and you emphasize the importance of clearly communicating the imputation methods in any publications or reports resulting from the analysis.

7. Results and Impact:

Upon completing the analysis, you find that the imputed data has strengthened the dataset, allowing for a more comprehensive assessment of the drug's effectiveness. Sensitivity analyses are conducted to gauge the robustness of results under different imputation scenarios, providing a clearer picture of the uncertainties associated with missing data.

8. Future Trends:

As a forward-looking data analyst, you explore emerging trends in missing data handling, including the integration of advanced machine learning models for imputation and the potential benefits of incorporating patient-reported outcomes to enhance imputation accuracy.

9. Implications for Clinical Practice:

The successful handling of missing data in this clinical study has implications for future research and clinical practice. It underscores the importance of addressing missing data systematically, recognizing the nuances introduced by different missing data mechanisms, and applying a combination of imputation strategies for a more comprehensive and robust analysis.

This example illustrates the practical application of handling missing data in a real-world scenario, emphasizing the importance of a thoughtful and transparent approach to ensure the validity and reliability of study findings.

2.2.2 Removing Outliers

Data cleaning and preprocessing are essential steps in the data analysis pipeline, and addressing outliers is a critical component of ensuring the integrity and reliability of the analytical process. In this section, we delve into the challenges posed by outliers, explore various methods for their detection and removal, and discuss the implications of outlier handling on downstream analyses.

1. Understanding Outliers:

- Outliers are data points that deviate significantly from the general pattern of the dataset. They can distort statistical analyses, impact the accuracy of models, and lead to biased conclusions. Identifying and appropriately handling outliers is crucial for obtaining meaningful insights from data.

2. Types of Outliers:

- *Global Outliers:* Data points that are outliers across the entire dataset, often representing extreme values relative to the overall distribution.

- *Contextual Outliers:* Data points that are outliers within a specific subset or context, emphasizing the importance of considering domain knowledge when assessing outlier status.

3. Methods for Outlier Detection:

- *Visual Inspection:* Utilize visualizations such as box plots, scatter plots, and histograms to identify potential outliers. Visual inspection is an effective initial step, especially when exploring the overall distribution of variables.

- *Statistical Methods:* Leverage statistical techniques such as z-scores, standard deviations, and the interquartile range (IQR) to quantify the degree of deviation of data points from the mean. Data points beyond a certain threshold may be flagged as potential outliers.

- *Machine Learning Models:* Train models, such as isolation forests or one-class SVMs, to identify observations that deviate from the expected patterns in the data. Machine learning-based approaches can capture complex relationships and dependencies.

- *Domain Knowledge:* Incorporate domain expertise to identify outliers that may be meaningful or indicative of specific conditions. This qualitative approach is valuable in understanding the context of the data.

4. Approaches to Removing Outliers:

- *Trimming:* Remove a fixed percentage of data points from the tails of the distribution. While straightforward, this method may discard potentially valuable information.

- *Winsorizing:* Capping extreme values by replacing them with values at a specified percentile. Winsorizing retains the overall distribution while mitigating the impact of outliers.

- *Transformation:* Apply mathematical transformations, such as log or square root, to data to reduce the influence of outliers. Transformations can make the data more amenable to analysis.

- *Imputation:* Replace outlier values with imputed values based on statistical measures or machine learning models. Imputation ensures that extreme values do not unduly influence subsequent analyses.

5. Impact of Outlier Removal on Data Distribution:

- Removing outliers alters the distribution of variables, affecting measures of central tendency, dispersion, and skewness. Analysts must carefully evaluate the implications of outlier removal on the overall shape and characteristics of the data.

6. Ethical Considerations:

- Transparently document the criteria and methods used for outlier removal to ensure reproducibility and ethical reporting. Acknowledge the potential influence of outlier handling on study outcomes and interpretations.

7. Case Studies:

- Explore practical case studies where the removal of outliers significantly impacted analytical results. Understand the decision-making process and the rationale behind outlier handling in specific contexts.

8. Advanced Techniques for Outlier Handling:

- Delve into advanced methods, including robust statistical techniques, machine learning algorithms for outlier detection, and ensemble approaches. Assess the applicability of these techniques in diverse analytical scenarios.

9. Outlier Detection in Time Series Data:

- Discuss unique considerations and techniques for identifying outliers in time series data. Time-dependent trends and seasonality pose specific challenges that require tailored approaches.

10. Conclusion: Striking the Balance in Outlier Handling:

- Outlier removal is a nuanced process that requires a delicate balance between preserving meaningful data and ensuring analytical robustness. This section equips analysts with a toolkit of methods, considerations, and ethical guidelines for effectively addressing outliers in diverse datasets. As data analysts navigate the intricate landscape of outlier detection and removal, a thoughtful and informed approach enhances the validity and reliability of analytical outcomes.

Example Scenario: Removing Outliers in Financial Data Analysis

Let's consider a scenario where you are tasked with analyzing a dataset containing daily stock prices for a portfolio of diverse financial assets. The dataset spans several years and includes variables such as daily closing prices, trading volumes, and price-to-earnings ratios.

1. Identifying Outliers:

Upon initial exploration, you notice extreme spikes in the daily closing prices for certain stocks, well beyond the typical fluctuations observed in the majority of the assets. These anomalies could potentially distort statistical measures and impact the accuracy of any predictive models.

2. Types of Outliers:

In this financial context, outliers can take various forms. Global outliers may represent extreme price changes affecting the entire market, while contextual outliers might be specific to individual stocks due to corporate events such as earnings reports or mergers.

3. Methods for Outlier Detection:

- **Visual Inspection:** Plotting time series graphs and scatter plots allows for visual identification of days with unusually high or low closing prices.

- **Statistical Methods:** Applying statistical measures like z-scores or the interquartile range helps quantify the deviation of daily closing prices from the mean or median.

- **Machine Learning Models:** Training machine learning models, such as an isolation forest, can automatically identify days with atypical price movements based on historical patterns.

4. Approaches to Removing Outliers:

- **Winsorizing:** Given the potential impact of extreme price changes on subsequent analyses, you decide to winsorize the daily closing prices. Any values beyond the 95th percentile are capped to the 95th percentile, preserving the general distribution of prices while mitigating the impact of extreme fluctuations.

- **Imputation:** For cases where extreme price changes might be indicative of genuine market events, you opt for imputation. Outliers are replaced with values predicted using a time-series forecasting model, considering factors such as historical prices, trading volumes, and relevant financial indicators.

5. Impact on Data Distribution:

- After outlier removal, the distribution of daily closing prices becomes more consistent, with reduced volatility in the dataset. This allows for a clearer representation of typical market behavior and trends.

6. Ethical Considerations:

- Transparently document the outlier removal process, highlighting the rationale behind choosing specific methods. Acknowledge that outlier handling can influence investment decisions and communicate these considerations in reports to maintain transparency.

7. Results and Implications:

- Analyzing the dataset post-outlier removal reveals more stable trends and facilitates the development of predictive models that are less influenced by extreme price fluctuations. The refined dataset enhances the reliability of financial forecasts and investment strategies.

8. Advanced Techniques:

- Explore the use of advanced techniques such as robust statistical methods or deep learning models for outlier detection, especially in dynamic financial markets where patterns may evolve over time.

9. Outlier Detection in Time Series Data:

- Discuss specific challenges in identifying outliers in time series data, where trends, seasonality, and external events can contribute to fluctuations. Highlight techniques tailored to address these challenges.

10. Conclusion: Balancing Prudence and Realism in Financial Data Analysis:

- Removing outliers in financial data demands a careful balance between prudence and realism. This example demonstrates the application of various methods to enhance the reliability of financial analyses while considering the nuances of market dynamics. As financial analysts navigate the complexities of outlier handling, a strategic approach ensures that insights drawn from data are robust, actionable, and aligned with ethical standards.

2.2.3 Standardizing and Normalizing Data

Data standardization and normalization are integral steps in the data cleaning and preprocessing phase, aimed at enhancing the comparability, interpretability, and performance of analytical models. In this section, we explore the concepts of standardization and normalization, their significance, and the methodologies employed to achieve these transformations.

1. Understanding Standardization and Normalization:

- **Standardization:** Standardization involves rescaling data to have a mean (average) of 0 and a standard deviation of 1. This ensures that the transformed data follows a standard normal distribution.

- **Normalization:** Normalization scales data to a specific range, typically between 0 and 1. It is particularly useful when the original dataset has varying scales, preventing certain features from dominating others during analyses.

2. The Importance of Standardization and Normalization:

- **Enhanced Model Performance:** Many machine learning algorithms, such as support vector machines and k-nearest neighbors, rely on distance measures. Standardizing or normalizing features ensures that all variables contribute equally to distance calculations, preventing the dominance of features with larger scales.

- **Convergence in Optimization:** Standardization aids in quicker convergence during optimization processes, especially in algorithms like gradient descent, where consistent scales facilitate a more straightforward search for the optimal solution.

- **Interpretability and Comparability:** Standardized and normalized data is more interpretable, as values are on a comparable scale. This is crucial when interpreting coefficients in linear models or comparing the impact of different features on model outcomes.

3. Standardization Process:

- **Z-Score Standardization:** The z-score is calculated for each data point by subtracting the mean and dividing by the standard deviation. This process results in a distribution with a mean of 0 and a standard deviation of 1.

- **Mathematical Representation:** The formula for standardizing a variable x is given by: $z = \frac{(x - \mu)}{\sigma}$, where \(\mu \) is the mean and \(\sigma \) is the standard deviation.

4. Normalization Process:

- **Min-Max Scaling:** In this method, each data point is scaled to a value between 0 and 1 based on the minimum and maximum values in the dataset.

- **Mathematical Representation:** The formula for normalizing a variable x is given by:

$$x_{\text{normalized}} = \frac{(x - \min(x))}{(\max(x) - \min(x))}.$$

5. Handling Skewed Distributions:

- Standardization and normalization can also be beneficial when dealing with skewed distributions, ensuring that the transformed data adheres to a more symmetric and interpretable form.

6. Practical Considerations:

- **Feature Selection:** Consider whether all features should be standardized or normalized. In some cases, only specific features may benefit from these transformations.

- **Impact on Interpretation:** While standardization and normalization facilitate model performance, it's essential to communicate the implications of these transformations to stakeholders for accurate interpretation of results.

7. Case Studies:

- **Regression Analysis:** Explore a case study where standardization improves the interpretability of regression coefficients, allowing for a more nuanced understanding of feature importance.

- **Clustering Algorithms:** Investigate how normalization enhances the performance of clustering algorithms, ensuring that clusters are formed based on the inherent patterns in the data rather than the scale of features.

8. Advanced Techniques:

- **Robust Scaling:** Introduce robust scaling as an alternative to standardization, especially when dealing with datasets containing outliers. Robust scaling uses the median and interquartile range for rescaling.

- **Power Transformations:** Explore the use of power transformations, such as the Box-Cox transformation, for normalizing data with non-constant variance.

9. Ethical Considerations:

- **Transparent Reporting:** Emphasize the importance of transparently reporting standardization and normalization procedures in research findings, ensuring that stakeholders are informed about the impact on data interpretation.

10. Conclusion: Striking the Right Balance in Data Transformation:

- The art of standardizing and normalizing data involves striking a delicate balance between enhancing model performance and maintaining the interpretability of results. As data analysts navigate the complexities of data cleaning and preprocessing, a thoughtful approach to standardization and normalization ensures that analytical models are robust, reliable, and aligned with the objectives of the analysis.

2.3 Statistical Foundations for Data Analysis

2.3.1 Probability Distributions

Probability distributions form the bedrock of statistical thinking, providing a framework to model uncertainty and randomness in data. In this section, we delve into the fundamentals of probability distributions, exploring their types, properties, and applications in data analysis.

1. Understanding Probability Distributions:

- **Definition:** Probability distributions describe the likelihood of different outcomes in a random experiment. They assign probabilities to various events, reflecting the uncertainty inherent in many real-world scenarios.

- **Random Variables:** Central to probability distributions are random variables, which represent numerical outcomes of random processes. These variables can be discrete, taking on distinct values, or continuous, encompassing a range of values.

2. Types of Probability Distributions:

- **Discrete Distributions:**

  - **Bernoulli Distribution:** Models a binary outcome, such as success/failure or yes/no, with a single parameter representing the probability of success.

  - **Binomial Distribution:** Generalizes the Bernoulli distribution to describe the number of successes in a fixed number of independent Bernoulli trials.

- **Continuous Distributions:**

- **Normal Distribution (Gaussian):** Characterized by a bell-shaped curve, the normal distribution is ubiquitous in nature and describes many phenomena due to the Central Limit Theorem.

- **Exponential Distribution:** Models the time between events in a Poisson process, often used in reliability and queuing theory.

- **Uniform Distribution:** Assumes all values within a specified range are equally likely.

- **Multimodal Distributions:**

- **Bimodal and Multimodal Distributions:** Occur when a dataset exhibits two or more distinct modes or peaks. Understanding multimodal distributions is essential for capturing complex patterns in data.

3. Properties of Probability Distributions:

- **Mean (Expected Value):** Represents the center of a distribution, calculated by summing the products of values and their probabilities.

- **Variance and Standard Deviation:** Measure the spread or dispersion of a distribution. The standard deviation is the square root of the variance.

- **Skewness and Kurtosis:** Capture asymmetry and tail characteristics of a distribution, providing insights into its shape.

4. Real-World Applications:

- **Financial Markets:** Probability distributions model asset returns, aiding in risk assessment and portfolio management.

- **Quality Control:** Distributions help analyze variations in manufacturing processes, guiding decisions to maintain product quality.

- **Healthcare:** Used in clinical trials to model the distribution of patient responses to treatments.

5. Probability Distributions in Hypothesis Testing:

- Probability distributions play a pivotal role in hypothesis testing, where the distribution of a test statistic under a null hypothesis determines the probability of observing the data.

6. Simulation and Monte Carlo Methods:

- Probability distributions are harnessed in simulation studies and Monte Carlo methods to model uncertainty, facilitating the generation of random samples for statistical analysis.

7. Advanced Concepts:

- **Beta Distribution:** Applied in Bayesian statistics, representing a distribution of probabilities.

- **Poisson Distribution:** Models the number of events occurring within fixed intervals, commonly used in queuing theory and reliability engineering.

8. Practical Considerations:

- **Choosing the Right Distribution:** The choice of a probability distribution should align with the characteristics of the data and the objectives of the analysis.

- **Transformations:** Transforming data to conform to a specific distribution is common in statistical analyses to meet assumptions of parametric tests.

9. Ethical Considerations:

- **Transparent Reporting:** Communicate the assumptions and limitations associated with chosen probability distributions, ensuring transparency in statistical analyses.

10. Conclusion: Navigating Uncertainty with Probability Distributions:

- Probability distributions serve as a powerful tool in the data analyst's toolkit, allowing for a nuanced understanding of uncertainty and variability. As analysts navigate through statistical foundations, a solid grasp of probability distributions enhances the accuracy and reliability of inferences drawn from data, fostering a more informed and robust data analysis process.

Example Dataset Illustrating Probability Distributions

Let's consider a dataset related to the daily sales of a retail store. This dataset captures the number of items sold each day over a span of one month. Analyzing this dataset allows us to illustrate various probability distributions commonly encountered in real-world scenarios.

1. Discrete Distributions:

- Bernoulli Distribution (Binary Outcome):

- Suppose we define a "successful day" as a day where the store sells more than a certain threshold, say 50 items. The Bernoulli distribution can model the probability of having a successful day (success = 1, failure = 0) based on this criterion.

- Binomial Distribution (Number of Successes in Trials):

- If we categorize days as successful or not based on the threshold, the binomial distribution can represent the likelihood of achieving a specific number of successful days out of the total observed days in the month.

2. Continuous Distributions:

- Normal Distribution (Daily Sales):

- Assume that the daily sales follow a normal distribution, with the mean representing the average daily sales and the standard deviation indicating the variability. The Central Limit Theorem suggests that the sum of a large number of independent, identically distributed random variables (daily sales) tends to follow a normal distribution.

- Exponential Distribution (Time between Sales):

- If we are interested in modeling the time between consecutive sales events, the exponential distribution can be employed. It characterizes the probability density function of the time until the next sale occurs.

- Uniform Distribution (Sales Targets):

- Consider a scenario where the store sets a sales target range for a day (e.g., 30 to 70 items). The uniform distribution can model the likelihood of achieving different sales values within this specified range.

3. Multimodal Distribution:

- Bimodal Distribution (Special Sale Days):

- Introduce the concept of special sale days, where the store experiences exceptionally high or low sales. This leads to a bimodal distribution, capturing the distinct modes associated with regular and special sale days.

4. Skewed Distribution:

- Skewed Distribution (Customer Traffic):

- If the number of customers entering the store per day is considered, it might follow a skewed distribution. For instance, days with special promotions could lead to an influx of customers, resulting in a positively skewed distribution.

5. Hypothetical Data Scenario:

- **Scenario:** On a particular day, the store unexpectedly sells a record-breaking number of items, leading to a potential outlier in the dataset.

- **Impact:** This outlier could influence the skewness and kurtosis of the distribution, highlighting the importance of outlier detection and management in data analysis.

6. Simulation for Future Sales:

- **Monte Carlo Simulation:** By leveraging probability distributions, especially the observed distributions in the dataset, analysts can perform Monte Carlo simulations to forecast future sales scenarios. This can aid in strategic decision-making and resource allocation.

7. Practical Considerations:

- **Transformations:** Applying logarithmic transformations to the sales data might be necessary to stabilize variances and meet assumptions of certain probability distributions.

- **Validating Assumptions:** Before choosing a distribution, analysts should assess whether the data aligns with the assumptions of the selected distribution.

8. Ethical Considerations:

- **Communication:** Transparently communicate the assumptions made in selecting and applying probability distributions to avoid misinterpretations of results.

In summary, the daily sales dataset serves as a versatile example to illustrate the application of various probability distributions in data analysis, showcasing their utility in capturing different aspects of uncertainty and variability in real-world scenarios.

2.3.2 Hypothesis Testing

Hypothesis testing is a cornerstone of statistical inference, providing a systematic framework for making decisions about population parameters based on sample data. In this section, we delve into the intricacies of hypothesis testing, exploring its principles, common methodologies, and practical applications in data analysis.

1. Understanding Hypothesis Testing:

- **Definition:** Hypothesis testing is a statistical method used to make inferences about population parameters by evaluating competing hypotheses about the underlying data distribution.

- **Two Hypotheses:**
  - **Null Hypothesis (H0):** Assumes no effect or no difference. It serves as a baseline for comparison.
  - **Alternative Hypothesis (H1 or Ha):** Asserts the presence of an effect or difference.

2. Key Components of Hypothesis Testing:

- **Test Statistic:** A numerical summary derived from sample data used to assess the evidence against the null hypothesis.

- **P-Value:** The probability of obtaining a test statistic as extreme as or more extreme than the one observed, assuming the null hypothesis is true.

- **Significance Level (Alpha):** The predetermined threshold below which the p-value leads to the rejection of the null hypothesis. Common choices include 0.05 and 0.01.

3. Steps in Hypothesis Testing:

- **Formulation of Hypotheses:** Clearly state the null and alternative hypotheses based on the research question.

- **Selection of Significance Level:** Choose a significance level that reflects the desired balance between Type I and Type II errors.

- **Data Collection:** Gather and prepare the sample data in accordance with the research design.

- **Calculation of Test Statistic:** Use appropriate statistical tests (e.g., t-test, chi-square test) to compute the test statistic.

- **P-Value Calculation:** Determine the probability of observing the test statistic under the null hypothesis.

- **Decision Rule:** If the p-value is less than the significance level, reject the null hypothesis; otherwise, fail to reject the null hypothesis.

- **Conclusion:** Communicate the findings and implications based on the results of hypothesis testing.

4. Common Types of Hypothesis Tests:

- **t-Test:** Used for comparing means of two groups, often employed in scenarios involving continuous data.

- **Chi-Square Test:** Applied for assessing the association between categorical variables.

- **ANOVA (Analysis of Variance):** Utilized when comparing means across multiple groups.

- **Paired Sample t-Test:** Specifically designed for paired or matched data.

5. Practical Applications in Data Analysis:

- **Marketing Studies:** Hypothesis testing can evaluate the effectiveness of marketing campaigns by comparing customer response metrics before and after implementation.

- **Medical Research:** Assess the impact of a new drug by comparing patient outcomes between the treatment and control groups.

- **Quality Control:** Verify whether changes in manufacturing processes lead to statistically significant improvements in product quality.

6. Interpretation of Results:

- **Rejecting the Null Hypothesis:** Indicates sufficient evidence to support the alternative hypothesis.

- **Failing to Reject the Null Hypothesis:** Suggests insufficient evidence to make conclusions in favor of the alternative hypothesis.

7. Challenges and Considerations:

- **Type I and Type II Errors:** Acknowledge the trade-off between incorrectly rejecting a true null hypothesis (Type I error) and failing to reject a false null hypothesis (Type II error).

- **Sample Size:** Consider the impact of sample size on the power of hypothesis tests, ensuring adequate statistical power to detect meaningful effects.

8. Real-World Case Studies:

- **A/B Testing in E-Commerce:** Illustrate how hypothesis testing is applied in A/B testing scenarios to assess changes in user behavior.

- **Clinical Trials:** Explore the critical role of hypothesis testing in determining the efficacy of new medical treatments.

9. Advanced Concepts:

- **Bayesian Hypothesis Testing:** Introduce Bayesian approaches to hypothesis testing, emphasizing the incorporation of prior knowledge.

- **Multiple Testing Corrections:** Discuss strategies to address the issue of inflated Type I error rates in scenarios involving multiple hypothesis tests.

10. Ethical Considerations:

- **Transparent Reporting:** Emphasize the importance of transparently reporting the methodology, results, and limitations of hypothesis testing to ensure ethical and accurate interpretation.

In conclusion, hypothesis testing stands as a powerful tool in the data analyst's toolkit, guiding decision-making processes and providing a structured approach to drawing meaningful inferences from sample data. A solid understanding of hypothesis testing empowers analysts to navigate the complexities of data analysis with statistical rigor and clarity.

Illustrative Example of Hypothesis Testing in Retail

Consider a scenario in the retail industry where a store aims to assess the impact of a new layout design on customer spending behavior. The store's management is interested in knowing whether the new layout has a significant effect on the average purchase amount per customer.

1. Formulating Hypotheses:

- **Null Hypothesis (H0):** The new layout has no effect on the average purchase amount per customer.

- **Alternative Hypothesis (Ha):** The new layout significantly influences the average purchase amount per customer.

2. Data Collection:

- The store collects data on the average purchase amounts from a random sample of customers under both the old and new layout conditions.

3. Selection of Significance Level:

- A significance level (alpha) of 0.05 is chosen, implying that the store is willing to accept a 5% chance of making a Type I error.

4. Calculation of Test Statistic:

- Assuming the data is normally distributed, a paired sample t-test is conducted to compare the average purchase amounts before and after the layout change.

5. P-Value Calculation:

- The computed p-value is, for instance, 0.03, indicating the probability of observing the obtained difference in average purchase amounts if the null hypothesis is true.

6. Decision Rule:

- As the p-value (0.03) is less than the significance level (0.05), the store decides to reject the null hypothesis.

7. Conclusion:

- The rejection of the null hypothesis suggests that there is sufficient evidence to infer that the new layout has a significant effect on the average purchase amount per customer.

8. Real-World Implications:

- Armed with this statistical insight, the store may choose to implement the new layout across all branches, anticipating increased revenue based on the observed positive impact on customer spending.

9. Ethical Considerations:

- The store ensures transparent reporting of the hypothesis testing process, emphasizing the limitations and potential sources of bias in the study. This ethical approach enhances the credibility of the findings.

10. Further Analysis:

- Post-implementation, the store continues to monitor and analyze customer spending patterns to validate the long-term impact of the new layout, fostering an iterative and data-driven decision-making process.

In this example, hypothesis testing serves as a pivotal tool for the retail store, allowing it to make informed decisions about implementing changes based on statistical evidence. The application of hypothesis testing extends beyond this scenario, showcasing its versatility in addressing various research questions and informing strategic choices across industries.

2.3.3 Confidence Intervals

Confidence intervals (CIs) are an essential statistical tool that provides a range of values within which we can reasonably expect a population parameter to lie. In this section, we will explore the concept of confidence intervals, their construction, interpretation, and practical applications in data analysis.

1. Understanding Confidence Intervals:

- **Definition:** A confidence interval is a range of values constructed from sample data that is likely to include the true value of a population parameter. It quantifies the uncertainty associated with estimating population parameters based on sample statistics.

- **Representation:** A confidence interval is typically expressed as (point estimate - margin of error, point estimate + margin of error).

2. Key Components of Confidence Intervals:

- **Point Estimate:** The sample statistic (e.g., mean, proportion) used as the best estimate of the population parameter.

- **Margin of Error:** The range within which we expect the true population parameter to fall. It is determined by the chosen level of confidence and the variability of the sample data.

- **Level of Confidence:** The probability that the calculated confidence interval contains the true population parameter. Commonly chosen levels are 90%, 95%, and 99%.

4. Interpretation of Confidence Intervals:

- **Example:** A 95% confidence interval for the mean daily sales of a product is (\$5000, \$5500). This suggests that we are 95% confident that the true mean daily sales fall within this range.

- **No Overlapping Intervals:** When comparing confidence intervals, if they do not overlap, it indicates a statistically significant difference between the corresponding population parameters.

5. Practical Applications:

- **Market Research:** Constructing confidence intervals for customer satisfaction scores helps businesses estimate the true level of customer satisfaction within a certain range.

- **Quality Control:** Confidence intervals for manufacturing process parameters (e.g., mean thickness of a coating) assist in ensuring product quality.

- **Political Polling:** In election polling, confidence intervals for candidate support percentages convey the uncertainty associated with the estimates.

6. Impact of Sample Size:

- **Larger Sample Sizes:** As the sample size increases, the margin of error decreases, leading to narrower confidence intervals.

- **Small Sample Sizes:** Smaller sample sizes result in wider confidence intervals, reflecting higher uncertainty.

7. Real-World Case Studies:

- **Economic Forecasting:** Discuss how confidence intervals are utilized in predicting economic indicators such as GDP growth rates.

- **Medical Research:** Explore the application of confidence intervals in estimating the effectiveness of a new drug in clinical trials.

8. Limitations and Considerations:

- **Assumptions:** Confidence intervals rely on assumptions such as normality of data and known population standard deviations.

- **Interpretation Caution**: Emphasize caution in interpreting confidence intervals, avoiding the common misconception that there is a 95% probability that the true parameter lies within the interval.

9. Advanced Concepts:

- **Bootstrapping:** Introduce the concept of bootstrap confidence intervals, which rely on resampling techniques and do not assume specific distributions.

- **Bayesian Intervals:** Discuss Bayesian credibility intervals as an alternative approach, incorporating prior knowledge into interval estimation.

10. Ethical Considerations:

- **Transparent Reporting:** Emphasize the importance of clearly communicating the methodology used in constructing confidence intervals to facilitate informed decision-making and avoid misinterpretation.

In conclusion, confidence intervals are a powerful tool in data analysis, providing a nuanced perspective on the range of plausible values for population parameters. A solid understanding of confidence intervals empowers analysts to convey the uncertainty inherent in statistical estimates and make informed decisions based on reliable information.

Illustrative Example of Confidence Intervals in Market Research

Imagine a market research firm conducting a survey to estimate the average satisfaction score of customers regarding a newly launched product. The research team collects a random sample of 200 customers and obtains satisfaction scores on a scale of 1 to 10. The goal is to construct a 95% confidence interval for the true average satisfaction score of all customers.

1. Data Collection:

- A random sample of 200 customers provides satisfaction scores, yielding a sample mean of 8.2 and a sample standard deviation (\(s\)) of 1.5.

2. Formulation of Confidence Interval:

- For the average satisfaction score, the confidence interval is constructed using the formula:

$\bar{x} \pm Z\left(\frac{s}{\sqrt{n}}\right)$ Assuming a normal distribution, for a 95% confidence interval, the critical value (Z) is approximately 1.96.

3. Calculation:

- Substituting the values:

- Substituting the values:

$$8.2 \pm 1.96 \left(\frac{1.5}{\sqrt{200}} \right)$$

4. Interpretation:

- The resulting confidence interval might be (7.95, 8.45). This implies that the market research firm is 95% confident that the true average satisfaction score of all customers falls within this range.

5. Decision-Making:

- If the product team aims to assess whether the satisfaction score exceeds a specific threshold (e.g., 8), they can use the confidence interval to make informed decisions.

6. Overlapping Intervals:

- Suppose another survey is conducted later, resulting in a 95% confidence interval of (7.90, 8.40). The lack of overlap suggests a potential significant difference in satisfaction scores between the two periods.

7. Impact of Sample Size:

- If the sample size were smaller (e.g., 50 customers), the confidence interval would be wider, reflecting greater uncertainty about the true average satisfaction score.

8. Transparency in Reporting:

- In conveying the results to stakeholders, the market research firm transparently reports the methodology, assumptions, and the implications of the confidence interval.

9. Real-World Application:

- The company can use this information to make strategic decisions, such as refining marketing strategies or addressing specific aspects of the product that may influence customer satisfaction.

10. Ethical Considerations:

- Emphasizing the importance of transparent reporting helps avoid misinterpretations and ensures that stakeholders understand the inherent uncertainty associated with the estimated confidence interval.

This example illustrates how confidence intervals provide a practical tool for market researchers, allowing them to estimate population parameters with a level of confidence and make data-driven decisions in a dynamic business environment.

CHAPTER III
Advanced Data Analysis Techniques

3.1 Regression Analysis

3.1.1 Simple Linear Regression

Regression analysis is a powerful statistical method employed in data analysis to understand the relationship between a dependent variable and one or more independent variables. This chapter delves into various aspects of regression analysis, starting with the foundational concept of simple linear regression.

3.1.1 Simple Linear Regression

Introduction to Simple Linear Regression:

Simple linear regression is the most basic form of regression analysis, examining the relationship between two continuous variables. In this method, one variable, known as the dependent variable, is predicted based on the values of another variable, the independent variable. The goal is to establish a linear equation that best describes the relationship, allowing for accurate predictions and insights into the nature of the association.

The Mathematical Framework:

The fundamental equation of simple linear regression is represented as:

$$Y - \beta_0 + \beta_1 X + \varepsilon$$

Here, \(Y\) is the dependent variable, \(X\) is the independent variable, \(\beta_0\) is the y-intercept, \(\beta_1\) is the slope, and \(\varepsilon\) represents the error term. The objective is to estimate the values of \(\beta_0\) and \(\beta_1\) that minimize the sum of squared differences between the observed and predicted values.

Assumptions of Simple Linear Regression:

To ensure the validity of the results, several assumptions must be satisfied in simple linear regression. These include linearity, independence, homoscedasticity, and normality of errors. Understanding and validating these assumptions are crucial steps in the analysis process.

Interpreting Regression Coefficients:

In simple linear regression, \(\beta_0\) represents the intercept, indicating the value of \(Y\) when \(X\) is zero. Meanwhile, \(\beta_1\) signifies the slope, denoting the change in \(Y\) for a unit change in \(X\). A thorough interpretation of these coefficients provides insights into the direction and strength of the relationship between the variables.

Model Evaluation and Validation:

Once the regression model is established, it is essential to assess its performance and validity. Various metrics, such as the coefficient of determination (R-squared), standard error of the estimate, and significance tests for regression coefficients, help evaluate the model's goodness of fit and generalizability to new data.

Practical Applications:

Simple linear regression finds application in diverse fields, from finance to healthcare. Understanding the relationship between variables allows analysts to make predictions, identify patterns, and make informed decisions. Case studies and real-world examples illustrate how simple linear regression is applied in different contexts, providing readers with practical insights into its utility.

Challenges and Considerations:

While simple linear regression is a valuable tool, it is not without challenges. Potential pitfalls, such as outliers, multicollinearity, and overfitting, should be addressed to ensure the reliability of the analysis. Strategies for handling these challenges and robustifying the model are discussed to equip analysts with the necessary skills.

Conclusion:

Simple linear regression serves as the foundation for more complex regression techniques explored in subsequent sections. Mastering this fundamental concept is crucial for analysts aiming to unravel the intricate relationships within their datasets, laying the groundwork for advanced data analysis techniques explored in the following chapters.

To illustrate the concept of simple linear regression, consider a scenario where we want to understand the relationship between the number of hours a student spends studying (independent variable, X) and their exam score (dependent variable, Y). The hypothesis is that the more hours a student dedicates to studying, the higher their exam score will be.

The Mathematical Framework:

The simple linear regression equation for this scenario would be:

$$\text{Exam Score} = \beta_0 + \beta_1 \times \text{Hours of Study} + \varepsilon$$

Here, β_0 is the y-intercept, representing the exam score when the student hasn't studied {Hours of Study} = 0, β_1 is the slope, indicating the change in the exam score for each additional hour of study, and \(\varepsilon\) is the error term accounting for unexplained variability.

Assumptions of Simple Linear Regression:

We assume that the relationship between hours of study and exam score is linear, the errors are independent and normally distributed, and the variability of scores is constant across all levels of study hours.

Interpreting Regression Coefficients:

If the estimated slope (\(\beta_1\)) is, for example, 5, it means that, on average, each additional hour of study is associated with a 5-point increase in the exam score. The y-intercept (\(\beta_0\)) provides the expected exam score when no study hours are logged.

Model Evaluation and Validation:

After fitting the regression model to our data, we use metrics like R-squared to assess how well the model explains the variability in exam scores. A high R-squared indicates a good fit, while significance tests help determine if the observed relationship is statistically significant.

Practical Applications:

In educational research, this simple linear regression model could guide administrators in advising students on optimal study hours for better exam performance. It provides actionable insights into the quantitative relationship between study time and academic success.

Challenges and Considerations:

Potential challenges may include outliers, where a few students significantly deviate from the general trend. Addressing outliers and ensuring that the assumptions of simple linear regression hold are crucial for accurate predictions.

Conclusion:

Through this example, we've demonstrated how simple linear regression can be applied to real-world scenarios, providing a foundation for more advanced regression techniques explored in subsequent sections. This foundational understanding equips data analysts with the tools to uncover valuable insights within their datasets.

3.1.2 Multiple Linear Regression

Building upon the foundation of simple linear regression, multiple linear regression extends the analysis to incorporate multiple independent variables. In this section, we explore the intricacies of modeling a relationship between a dependent variable and two or more predictors.

The Extended Model:

The multiple linear regression model can be expressed as:

$$Y = \beta_0 + \beta_1 X_1 + \beta_2 X_2 + \ldots + \beta_p X_p + \varepsilon$$

Here, \(Y\) is the dependent variable, \(X_1, X_2, ..., X_p\) are the independent variables, \(\beta_0\) is the intercept, \(\beta_1, \beta_2, ..., \beta_p\) are the respective coefficients, and \(\varepsilon\) represents the error term. The objective remains the same - to estimate the coefficients that minimize the difference between observed and predicted values.

Interpreting Coefficients in Multiple Linear Regression:

Understanding the coefficients in a multiple linear regression model is crucial for extracting meaningful insights. Each \(\beta\) coefficient represents the change in the dependent variable associated with a one-unit change in the corresponding independent variable, holding all other variables constant. This enables a nuanced analysis of how multiple factors collectively influence the outcome.

Assumptions and Considerations:

Multiple linear regression inherits some assumptions from simple linear regression, including linearity, independence, homoscedasticity, and normality of errors. Ensuring these assumptions are met is vital for the reliability of the model. Additionally, issues like multicollinearity (high correlation between independent variables) can pose challenges and require careful consideration.

Model Evaluation and Validation:

Evaluating the performance of a multiple linear regression model involves assessing its ability to explain the variability in the dependent variable. Techniques such as R-squared, adjusted R-squared, and significance tests for individual coefficients and the overall model aid in determining the model's effectiveness.

Practical Applications:

The versatility of multiple linear regression makes it applicable in various fields. For instance, in finance, it can be used to predict stock prices based on multiple economic indicators. In marketing, it might help understand the combined impact of advertising spending, product pricing, and promotional activities on sales.

Challenges and Strategies:

Navigating the challenges of multicollinearity, overfitting, or selecting relevant variables is integral to the success of multiple linear regression. Strategies such as feature selection, regularization techniques, and cross-validation are explored to enhance the model's robustness.

Conclusion:

Multiple linear regression emerges as a powerful tool in the data analyst's arsenal, enabling a more comprehensive exploration of relationships within datasets. As we delve into this advanced technique, we lay the groundwork for a deeper understanding of the intricate dynamics that govern diverse phenomena, setting the stage for further exploration in subsequent chapters.

Introduction to Multiple Linear Regression:

To illustrate the concept of multiple linear regression, let's consider a scenario in the realm of real estate. We want to predict house prices (Y) based on various factors, including the square footage of the house (X_1), the number of bedrooms (X_2), and the distance from the city center (X_3).

The Extended Model:

The multiple linear regression model for this scenario is:

$$\text{House Price} = \beta_0 + \beta_1 \times \text{Square Footage} + \beta_2 \times \text{Number of Bedrooms} + \beta_3 \times \text{Distance from City Center} + \varepsilon$$

Here, β_0 is the intercept, $\beta_1, \beta_2, \beta_3$ are the coefficients for square footage, number of bedrooms, and distance, respectively, and ε is the error term. The model aims to estimate the impact of each factor on the house price, considering all variables simultaneously.

Interpreting Coefficients in Multiple Linear Regression:

If β_1 is, for example, 150, it means that, on average, each additional square foot contributes $150 to the house price, holding the other variables constant. Similarly, β_2 and β_3 quantify the influence of bedrooms and distance on the house price.

Assumptions and Considerations:

Assumptions, such as linearity and independence, remain vital. In this context, linearity implies that the relationship between house price and each predictor is linear when other predictors are held constant. Checking for multicollinearity is crucial, as high correlations between, say, square footage and the number of bedrooms, can affect coefficient interpretations.

Model Evaluation and Validation:

After fitting the model, metrics like R-squared can provide insights into how well the combined variables explain the variability in house prices. Significance tests for individual coefficients help identify which factors significantly contribute to the model.

Practical Applications:

Real estate agents can leverage multiple linear regression to provide more accurate property valuations. Understanding how different factors influence house prices helps in setting competitive listing prices and advising clients on potential modifications to enhance property value.

Challenges and Strategies:

In this example, challenges may include handling categorical variables (e.g., neighborhood), ensuring the model's generalizability, and addressing outliers. Techniques like regularization or feature engineering can be employed to enhance the model's performance.

Conclusion:

This real estate example demonstrates the practical application of multiple linear regression, showcasing its versatility in capturing the interplay of multiple variables to predict outcomes. As we navigate through these examples, we equip data analysts with the tools to tackle complex real-world scenarios, paving the way for further exploration in advanced data analysis techniques.

3.1.3 Logistic Regression

While simple and multiple linear regression are designed for predicting continuous outcomes, logistic regression steps into the realm of classification problems, where the dependent variable is categorical. In this section, we explore logistic regression, a powerful tool for predicting binary outcomes.

The Logistic Regression Model:

Logistic regression utilizes the logistic function to model the probability of an event occurring. The logistic regression equation is given by:

$$P(Y=1) = \frac{1}{1+e^{-(\beta_0+\beta_1 X_1+\beta_2 X_2+\ldots+\beta_p X_p)}}$$

Here, $P(Y=1)$ is the probability of the event happening, $X_1, X_2, ..., X_p$ are the independent variables, and $\beta_0, \beta_1, \beta_2, ..., \beta_p$ are the coefficients to be estimated. The logistic function ensures that the predicted probabilities fall between 0 and 1.

Interpreting Logistic Regression Coefficients:

Unlike linear regression, interpreting logistic regression coefficients requires understanding odds ratios. If β_1 is, for instance, 0.5, it implies that a one-unit increase in X_1 increases the odds of the event happening by 50%. Conversely, if β_1 is -0.5, the odds decrease by 50%.

Assumptions and Considerations:

Logistic regression assumes that the relationship between the independent variables and the log-odds of the dependent variable is linear. Additionally, it requires the absence of multicollinearity among predictors and the need for a sufficient sample size for stable coefficient estimates.

Model Evaluation and Validation:

Evaluating the performance of a logistic regression model involves metrics such as accuracy, precision, recall, and the area under the receiver operating characteristic (ROC) curve. Understanding these metrics helps assess the model's ability to correctly classify instances.

Practical Applications:

Logistic regression finds widespread use in various fields, such as healthcare for predicting disease outcomes based on patient characteristics, or in marketing to predict customer churn. The binary nature of the dependent variable makes it applicable in scenarios where outcomes are either present or absent.

Challenges and Strategies:

Dealing with imbalanced datasets, selecting relevant predictors, and handling outliers are common challenges in logistic regression. Techniques like regularization, feature engineering, and adjusting decision thresholds are employed to enhance model performance.

Conclusion:

Logistic regression adds a valuable dimension to the data analyst's toolkit, allowing for the prediction of binary outcomes. As we delve into the intricacies of logistic regression, we equip analysts with the skills needed to navigate classification problems effectively. This understanding serves as a stepping stone for exploring more complex machine learning techniques in subsequent chapters.

3.2 Machine Learning for Data Analysts

3.2.1 Introduction to Machine Learning

Unlocking the Power of Machine Learning:

In the ever-evolving landscape of data analysis, machine learning emerges as a transformative force, enabling data analysts to extract patterns, make predictions, and automate decision-making processes. This section serves as a gateway to the vast realm of machine learning, introducing fundamental concepts and methodologies.

Defining Machine Learning:

At its core, machine learning is a subset of artificial intelligence that empowers systems to learn from data and improve their performance over time without explicit programming. The crux lies in developing algorithms that can generalize patterns from historical data to make predictions or decisions when faced with new, unseen data.

Types of Machine Learning:

Machine learning is broadly categorized into two main types: supervised and unsupervised learning.

- **Supervised Learning:** In supervised learning, the algorithm is trained on a labeled dataset, where the input data is paired with corresponding output labels. The goal is to learn a mapping function that can accurately predict the output for new, unseen inputs. Common supervised learning tasks include classification and regression.

- **Unsupervised Learning:** Unsupervised learning involves working with unlabeled data, where the algorithm explores the inherent structure and relationships within the data. Clustering and dimensionality reduction are typical tasks in unsupervised learning, aiding in pattern discovery and data exploration.

Key Components of Machine Learning:

Understanding the key components of machine learning is crucial for effective implementation.

- **Features and Labels:** Features are the input variables used to make predictions, while labels are the output values to be predicted. In supervised learning, the model learns the relationship between features and labels.

- **Training and Testing Data:** The dataset is typically divided into training and testing sets. The model is trained on the training set and evaluated on the testing set to assess its performance on unseen data.

- **Algorithms and Models:** Machine learning algorithms form the backbone of the predictive models. These algorithms vary based on the nature of the task, with popular ones including linear regression, decision trees, support vector machines, and neural networks.

Applications of Machine Learning:

Machine learning finds applications across diverse domains, revolutionizing industries and decision-making processes.

- **Healthcare:** Predicting disease outcomes, personalized medicine, and optimizing treatment plans.

- **Finance:** Credit scoring, fraud detection, and algorithmic trading.

- **Marketing:** Customer segmentation, recommendation systems, and targeted advertising.

- **Manufacturing:** Predictive maintenance, quality control, and supply chain optimization.

Challenges and Considerations:

While machine learning offers unprecedented capabilities, it comes with challenges, including overfitting, underfitting, and the interpretability of complex models. Striking a balance between model complexity and interpretability is crucial for practical applications.

Conclusion:

This introduction lays the groundwork for a comprehensive exploration of machine learning in subsequent sections. As we embark on this journey, data analysts will gain the knowledge and skills necessary to harness the potential of machine learning for extracting meaningful insights from complex datasets.

3.2.2 Supervised and Unsupervised Learning

Distinguishing Paths in Machine Learning:

In the vast landscape of machine learning, analysts traverse two fundamental paths—supervised learning and unsupervised learning. Each path offers unique insights and methodologies, catering to distinct analytical objectives. This section delves into the nuances of these approaches, unraveling their applications and methodologies.

1. Supervised Learning:

Guided by Labeled Data

Defining Supervised Learning:

Supervised learning revolves around the use of labeled datasets, where each observation has a corresponding output label. The objective is for the model to learn the mapping between input features and their corresponding labels, enabling it to make accurate predictions on new, unseen data.

Common Tasks in Supervised Learning:

- **Classification:** Assigning input data to predefined categories. For instance, spam detection, image recognition, and sentiment analysis are classic classification tasks.

- **Regression:** Predicting a continuous outcome. Examples include predicting house prices, stock values, or temperature.

Supervised Learning Workflow:

1. Data Collection: Acquiring a labeled dataset, where each data point has both input features and corresponding output labels.

2. Data Splitting: Dividing the dataset into training and testing sets to train the model on one portion and evaluate its performance on another.

3. Model Training: Employing algorithms such as decision trees, support vector machines, or neural networks to learn the relationship between features and labels.

4. Model Evaluation: Assessing the model's performance on the testing set using metrics like accuracy, precision, recall, and F1-score.

2. Unsupervised Learning:

Exploring the Unknown

Defining Unsupervised Learning:

Contrasting with its supervised counterpart, unsupervised learning operates on unlabeled data, seeking to uncover patterns, relationships, or hidden structures within the dataset without predefined output labels.

Common Tasks in Unsupervised Learning:

- **Clustering:** Grouping similar data points together based on intrinsic patterns. Examples include customer segmentation and document clustering.

- **Dimensionality Reduction:** Reducing the number of features while retaining essential information. Principal Component Analysis (PCA) is a common technique for dimensionality reduction.

Unsupervised Learning Workflow:

1. **Data Exploration:** Analyzing the structure and characteristics of the unlabeled dataset.

2. **Model Training:** Employing algorithms like k-means clustering or hierarchical clustering for grouping similar data points.

3. **Pattern Discovery:** Extracting meaningful patterns or structures from the data.

4. **Evaluation (if applicable):** Some unsupervised learning tasks may involve evaluating the quality of clusters or the effectiveness of dimensionality reduction.

Applications and Impact:

- **Supervised Learning:** Widely used in predictive modeling, supervised learning fuels applications in healthcare diagnostics, financial forecasting, and image recognition.

- **Unsupervised Learning:** Vital for data exploration and pattern recognition, unsupervised learning contributes to anomaly detection, recommendation systems, and understanding complex datasets.

Challenges and Considerations:

- **Supervised Learning:** Challenges include the need for labeled data, potential biases in training sets, and model interpretability for complex algorithms like neural networks.

- **Unsupervised Learning:** Challenges involve determining the optimal number of clusters, handling high-dimensional data, and the subjective nature of evaluating results.

Conclusion:

Navigating the realms of supervised and unsupervised learning equips data analysts with versatile tools for extracting valuable insights from diverse datasets. Understanding when to employ each approach is pivotal for addressing specific analytical goals, laying the foundation for more advanced machine learning endeavors explored in subsequent chapters.

3.2.3 Model Evaluation and Selection

Critical Steps in the Machine Learning Journey:

As data analysts embark on the machine learning journey, understanding the intricacies of model evaluation and selection becomes paramount. This section unravels the pivotal steps involved in assessing the performance of machine learning models and making informed choices for optimal results.

1. The Importance of Model Evaluation:

Model evaluation is the linchpin of the machine learning process, serving as the compass to navigate through the myriad of algorithms and parameters. It involves rigorously assessing a model's ability to generalize well to new, unseen data. The overarching goal is to ensure that the chosen model not only fits the training data well but also exhibits robust performance on real-world scenarios.

2. Key Metrics for Model Evaluation:

Several metrics provide a comprehensive view of a model's performance, depending on the nature of the task. Common metrics include:

- **Accuracy:** The proportion of correctly classified instances. Suitable for balanced datasets but may be misleading in imbalanced ones.

- **Precision:** The ratio of correctly predicted positive observations to the total predicted positives. Relevant when false positives are costly.

- **Recall (Sensitivity):** The ratio of correctly predicted positive observations to the total actual positives. Crucial when false negatives are costly.

- **F1-Score:** The harmonic mean of precision and recall, providing a balanced metric between the two.

- **Area Under the ROC Curve (AUC-ROC):** Evaluates the trade-off between true positive rate and false positive rate across various threshold values.

3. Cross-Validation Techniques:

Cross-validation is a pivotal practice to assess model performance robustly. Techniques like k-fold cross-validation involve dividing the dataset into k subsets, using k-1 folds for training and the remaining one for testing. This process is repeated k times, providing a more accurate estimation of a model's generalization performance.

4. Model Selection Strategies:

Selecting the right model involves considering factors such as model complexity, interpretability, and computational efficiency. Common strategies include:

- **Grid Search:** Systematically searching through a predefined hyperparameter grid to identify the optimal combination for model performance.

- **Random Search:** Randomly sampling from a hyperparameter space, offering computational efficiency while still exploring a diverse range of possibilities.

- **Ensemble Methods:** Combining predictions from multiple models to improve overall performance. Techniques like Random Forests and Gradient Boosting are popular ensemble methods.

5. Overfitting and Underfitting:

Balancing the trade-off between overfitting and underfitting is crucial. Overfitting occurs when a model learns noise in the training data and performs poorly on new data, while underfitting arises when a model is too simplistic and fails to capture the underlying patterns. Regularization techniques, such as L1 and L2 regularization, help mitigate overfitting.

6. Model Interpretability:

While sophisticated models may offer high predictive accuracy, their interpretability is often compromised. Striking a balance between complexity and interpretability is essential, especially in domains where transparency and explainability are paramount.

7. Real-world Considerations:

Finally, understanding the real-world implications of model decisions is crucial. Considering factors like ethical concerns, bias, and the impact of model predictions on decision-making processes is integral for responsible and informed model deployment.

Conclusion:

In the realm of machine learning, model evaluation and selection form the backbone of informed decision-making. As analysts navigate through diverse algorithms and techniques, mastering the art of evaluating models ensures that data-driven insights translate seamlessly into actionable outcomes. This comprehensive understanding paves the way for the exploration of advanced time series analysis techniques in the subsequent chapter.

3.3 Time Series Analysis

3.3.1 Decomposition

Unveiling Temporal Patterns:

Time series data, characterized by observations collected over time intervals, introduces a unique set of challenges and opportunities in data analysis. Decomposition is a fundamental technique within time series analysis that unravels the underlying components of a time series, providing valuable insights into trends, seasonality, and irregularities.

1. Understanding Decomposition:

Time series decomposition involves breaking down a time series into its constituent parts, typically comprising three main components:

- **Trend:** The long-term movement or general direction of the data. It captures the overall pattern, indicating whether the series is increasing, decreasing, or remaining relatively constant over time.

- **Seasonality:** The repetitive and predictable fluctuations within the data that occur at fixed intervals. Seasonal patterns are often influenced by external factors such as weather, holidays, or events specific to certain time periods.

- **Irregularity (Residuals):** The residual or remainder component represents the unexplained variability in the data after removing the trend and seasonal components. It encompasses random fluctuations, noise, or unexpected events.

2. Methods of Decomposition:

Several methods are employed for time series decomposition, with two common approaches being:

- **Additive Decomposition:** Expresses the time series as the sum of its trend, seasonal, and residual components. This method is suitable when the magnitude of the seasonality remains relatively constant across different levels of the time series.

$$Y(t) = \text{Trend}(t) + \text{Seasonality}(t) + \text{Residuals}(t)$$

- Multiplicative Decomposition: Represents the time series as the product of its trend, seasonal, and residual components. This approach is preferred when the seasonality exhibits proportional variation with the level of the time series.

$$Y(t) = \text{Trend}(t) \times \text{Seasonality}(t) \times \text{Residuals}(t)$$

3. Practical Applications:

Decomposition finds diverse applications across various industries and domains:

- **Business Forecasting:** Understanding the trend and seasonality of sales data aids in forecasting future sales, enabling businesses to make informed inventory and production decisions.

- **Economic Analysis:** Decomposing economic time series data helps economists discern long-term trends, cyclical patterns, and irregularities, facilitating better policy formulation.

- **Energy Consumption:** Identifying seasonal patterns and trends in energy consumption is crucial for optimizing resource allocation, managing peak loads, and planning infrastructure upgrades.

4. Challenges and Considerations:

While decomposition provides valuable insights, challenges may arise in the presence of outliers, sudden shocks, or irregularities that deviate from the assumed decomposition model. Robustness to unexpected events and appropriate handling of anomalies are critical considerations in time series analysis.

Conclusion:

Decomposition serves as a cornerstone in extracting meaningful information from time series data. By disentangling the temporal components, analysts gain a nuanced understanding of patterns, enabling accurate forecasting and strategic decision-making. This foundational knowledge sets the stage for delving deeper into advanced forecasting techniques in the subsequent section.

3.3.2 Forecasting Techniques

Peering into the Future:

Forecasting lies at the heart of time series analysis, empowering analysts to predict future values based on historical data patterns. This section delves into various forecasting techniques, unveiling methodologies to anticipate trends, make informed decisions, and optimize planning in diverse domains.

1. Time Series Forecasting:

Time series forecasting involves predicting future values or trends based on the observed historical data. This analytical process aids in understanding and adapting to the underlying patterns within the time series, ultimately facilitating proactive decision-making.

2. Common Forecasting Techniques:

Moving Averages:

- **Simple Moving Average (SMA):** Computes the average of a specified number of consecutive data points. It smoothens fluctuations, providing a clearer view of the trend.

- **Exponential Moving Average (EMA):** Assigns weights to recent observations, giving more significance to recent data points. Useful for capturing short-term trends.

ARIMA (AutoRegressive Integrated Moving Average):

- Combines autoregressive (AR) and moving average (MA) components. ARIMA models account for trends, seasonality, and irregularities in the time series data.

Prophet:

- Developed by Facebook, Prophet is a robust forecasting tool designed for datasets with strong seasonal patterns and multiple seasonality. It accommodates holidays, special events, and outliers.

Long Short-Term Memory (LSTM):

- A type of recurrent neural network (RNN), LSTM is effective for capturing long-term dependencies in time series data. It excels in scenarios with complex patterns and nonlinear relationships.

3. Model Selection and Evaluation:

Choosing the appropriate forecasting model is a critical step in the process. The selection depends on the nature of the time series, the presence of seasonality, and the desired balance between model complexity and interpretability.

Model Evaluation Metrics:

- Common metrics include Mean Absolute Error (MAE), Mean Squared Error (MSE), and Root Mean Squared Error (RMSE). These metrics quantify the accuracy of the forecasted values compared to the actual observations.

4. Practical Applications:

Time series forecasting finds applications across various industries, including:

- **Finance:** Predicting stock prices, currency exchange rates, and market trends.

- **Retail:** Forecasting demand for products, optimizing inventory levels, and planning promotions.

- **Energy:** Anticipating power consumption, optimizing resource allocation, and managing energy production.

5. Challenges and Considerations:

Challenges in time series forecasting include handling outliers, adapting to sudden shifts in data patterns, and choosing models that generalize well to unseen data. Additionally, the selection of appropriate forecasting horizons and the treatment of missing data require careful consideration.

Conclusion:

In mastering time series analysis, a profound understanding of forecasting techniques empowers analysts to unlock valuable insights from historical data. Whether predicting financial trends or optimizing resource allocation, the ability to foresee future developments enhances decision-making and strategic planning in a multitude of domains. As we conclude this exploration of time series analysis, the acquired knowledge serves as a stepping stone for further advanced applications in data analysis.

Illustrative Example: Predicting Monthly Sales

Context:

Consider a retail business that wants to optimize inventory management and streamline operations by predicting future monthly sales. The historical dataset includes monthly sales data spanning several years.

Forecasting Techniques Applied:

1. Moving Averages:

- Simple Moving Average (SMA):

- *Calculation:* For a 3-month SMA, the average of sales in the current month and the two preceding months.

- *Application:* Smoothes out short-term fluctuations, providing a clearer view of the overall sales trend.

- Exponential Moving Average (EMA):

- *Calculation:* Assigns more weight to recent sales data.

- *Application:* Useful for capturing short-term variations and adapting to changing sales patterns.

2. ARIMA (AutoRegressive Integrated Moving Average):

- *Methodology:* Combines autoregressive (AR) and moving average (MA) components.
- *Application:* Captures trends, seasonality, and irregularities in the sales data.

3. Prophet:

- *Features:* Accommodates holidays, special events, and multiple seasonality components.
- *Application:* Particularly effective for datasets with strong seasonal patterns.

4. Long Short-Term Memory (LSTM):

- *Type:* Recurrent Neural Network (RNN).
- *Strengths:* Excels in capturing long-term dependencies and nonlinear relationships in data.
- *Application:* Suitable for complex sales patterns with varying trends.

Model Selection and Evaluation:

The retail business evaluates the performance of each forecasting model using metrics such as Mean Absolute Error (MAE), Mean Squared Error (MSE), and Root Mean Squared Error (RMSE). This ensures that the chosen model aligns with the business objectives and accurately predicts future sales.

Practical Application:

The selected forecasting model is then deployed to predict monthly sales for the upcoming year. This information aids the retail business in optimizing inventory levels, planning marketing strategies, and enhancing overall operational efficiency.

Challenges and Considerations:

Challenges in this scenario may include handling sudden shifts in consumer behavior, adapting to external factors like economic changes, and ensuring the forecasting model's robustness to unforeseen events. Regular model reevaluation and updates are essential to maintaining accuracy.

Conclusion:

By leveraging time series forecasting techniques, the retail business gains actionable insights into future sales patterns. This enables strategic decision-making, ensures efficient resource allocation, and ultimately contributes to the business's success in a dynamic market environment. The example showcases the practical application of time series analysis in a real-world context, emphasizing the importance of selecting the right forecasting techniques for specific business needs.

CHAPTER IV
Data Governance and Ethics

4.1 Ensuring Data Quality and Integrity

4.1.1 Data Cleaning Best Practices

Navigating the Landscape of Data Cleaning:

Data cleaning is a pivotal phase in the data analysis process, aiming to enhance the quality and reliability of datasets. In this section, we explore a comprehensive set of best practices that empower analysts to navigate the intricacies of data cleaning, ensuring that the data under scrutiny is accurate, consistent, and ready for meaningful analysis.

1. Understanding Data Cleaning:

Data cleaning, also known as data cleansing or data scrubbing, involves the identification and rectification of errors, inconsistencies, and inaccuracies within a dataset. These errors may stem from various sources, including data entry mistakes, missing values, outliers, and formatting discrepancies.

2. Best Practices for Effective Data Cleaning:

Identifying and Handling Missing Values:

- *Techniques:* Imputation methods such as mean, median, or mode replacement, or advanced approaches like predictive modeling for missing value estimation.

- *Considerations:* Assess the impact of imputation on data integrity and choose methods that align with the nature of the missing data.

Handling Duplicate Records:

- *Approach:* Detect and remove duplicate entries based on key identifiers or specific attributes.

- *Considerations:* Be cautious not to inadvertently discard valid data, and consider the context to determine the criteria for identifying duplicates.

Outlier Detection and Treatment:

- *Identification:* Employ statistical methods or visualization techniques to identify outliers.

- *Treatment:* Decide whether to exclude outliers, transform them, or investigate and rectify any underlying issues in the data collection process.

Standardizing and Formatting:

- *Standardization:* Ensure consistent units, formats, and conventions across variables.

- *Formatting:* Utilize appropriate data types, convert categorical variables to a consistent format, and address any inconsistencies in coding.

Handling Inconsistent Data:

- *Identification:* Identify and resolve inconsistencies in categorical variables or data labels.

- *Resolution:* Develop a standardized coding system or reconcile conflicting entries to establish consistency.

Dealing with Typos and Spelling Errors:

- *Automated Tools:* Leverage spell-check tools and algorithms to identify and correct typos.

- *Manual Review:* Conduct a manual review for context-specific errors that automated tools may not capture.

3. Documentation and Reproducibility:

Documentation Practices:

- *Record-Keeping:* Maintain detailed documentation of data cleaning procedures, including the rationale for specific decisions.

- *Versioning:* Implement version control to track changes, ensuring transparency and reproducibility.

Reproducibility:

- *Scripting:* Transform data cleaning steps into scripts or code, allowing for easy replication and adaptation.

- *Validation:* Regularly validate and update cleaning procedures to accommodate evolving data requirements.

4. Collaborative Data Cleaning:

Communication:

- *Collaboration:* Foster communication between data analysts, domain experts, and stakeholders to address domain-specific nuances.

- *Feedback Loop:* Establish a feedback loop for ongoing improvements and corrections.

Training and Education:

- *Skill Enhancement:* Invest in training programs to enhance data cleaning skills across the team.

- *Documentation Training:* Emphasize the importance of clear and comprehensive documentation in collaborative environments.

5. Automated Data Cleaning Tools:

Utilization:

- *Explore Tools:* Investigate and implement automated tools for routine and repetitive cleaning tasks.

- *Validation:* Validate the output of automated tools to ensure accuracy and reliability.

Conclusion:

Embracing effective data cleaning practices is foundational to the success of any data analysis endeavor. By adopting a systematic approach, documenting procedures, and fostering collaboration, analysts can transform raw data into a reliable foundation for meaningful insights and informed decision-making. As we proceed through this chapter, the integration of robust data cleaning practices sets the stage for the ethical considerations essential in maintaining the integrity and privacy of data. **Chapter 4: Data Governance and Ethics**

Step 1: Initial Assessment of the Dataset

Begin by conducting a comprehensive assessment of the dataset to identify potential issues. This involves checking for missing values, outliers, duplicate records, inconsistent formatting, and any evident anomalies.

Step 2: Handling Missing Values

Techniques:

- Utilize mean, median, or mode imputation for numerical variables.
- Implement predictive modeling techniques for missing value estimation.
- Consider the impact of imputation methods on data integrity.

Example:

- Identify columns with missing values.
- Apply mean imputation to fill missing numerical values.
- Use predictive modeling for missing values in specific columns.

Step 3: Managing Duplicate Records

Approach:

- Identify duplicate entries based on key identifiers or relevant attributes.
- Develop criteria for distinguishing between genuine and erroneous duplicates.

Example:

- Identify and remove duplicate records based on unique customer IDs.
- Carefully assess criteria to avoid unintentional removal of valid data.

Step 4: Outlier Detection and Treatment

Identification:

- Utilize statistical methods or visualization techniques to identify outliers.
- Determine the threshold for defining outliers based on the nature of the data.

Treatment:

- Decide whether to exclude outliers, transform them, or investigate and address underlying issues.
- Document the rationale behind outlier treatment decisions.

Step 5: Standardizing and Formatting

Standardization:

- Ensure consistent units, formats, and conventions across variables.
- Convert categorical variables to a uniform format.

Formatting:

- Verify appropriate data types for each variable.
- Address any inconsistencies in coding and variable formats.

Step 6: Handling Inconsistent Data

Identification:

- Identify and resolve inconsistencies in categorical variables or data labels.
- Develop a standardized coding system to ensure consistency.

Resolution:

- Establish protocols for reconciling conflicting entries and maintaining consistency.
- Document the steps taken to address inconsistencies.

Step 7: Dealing with Typos and Spelling Errors

Automated Tools:

- Employ spell-check tools and algorithms to identify and correct typos.
- Leverage automated tools for systematic typo correction.

Manual Review:

- Conduct a manual review for context-specific errors not captured by automated tools.
- Document manual corrections made during the review process.

Step 8: Documentation and Reproducibility

Documentation Practices:

- Maintain detailed documentation of each data cleaning step.
- Include the rationale behind decisions and any assumptions made.

Reproducibility:

- Transform data cleaning steps into scripts or code for easy replication.
- Implement version control to track changes and updates.

Step 9: Collaborative Data Cleaning

Communication:

- Foster communication between team members, domain experts, and stakeholders.
- Establish channels for sharing insights, feedback, and updates.

Training and Education:

- Invest in training programs to enhance data cleaning skills across the team.
- Emphasize the importance of clear and comprehensive documentation.

Step 10: Automated Data Cleaning Tools

Utilization:

- Explore and implement automated tools for routine and repetitive cleaning tasks.
- Validate the output of automated tools to ensure accuracy.

Example:

- Implement an automated tool for detecting and correcting formatting inconsistencies.
- Validate the tool's output against a subset of manually reviewed records.

Conclusion:

By following these step-by-step data cleaning best practices, analysts can ensure that their datasets are reliable, accurate, and ready for meaningful analysis. The systematic approach, coupled with documentation and collaboration, sets the stage for ethical considerations in data analysis, which we will explore in the subsequent sections of this chapter.

4.1.2 Data Validation Techniques

Validating the Foundation: Techniques for Ensuring Data Integrity

Data validation is an integral aspect of the data analysis process, serving as a checkpoint to ensure that the data remains accurate, consistent, and compliant with predefined standards. This section delves into a comprehensive exploration of data validation techniques, providing analysts with the tools to validate and verify the integrity of their datasets.

1. Types of Data Validation:

Structural Validation:

- *Objective:* Ensures that the data structure conforms to predefined specifications.

- *Techniques:*

  - Schema validation: Verifies that the data follows a predefined schema or structure.

  - Format validation: Confirms that data adheres to the specified format (e.g., date format, alphanumeric patterns).

Semantic Validation:

- *Objective:* Validates the meaning and coherence of the data within and across datasets.

- *Techniques:*

  - Cross-field validation: Checks relationships between different fields to ensure consistency.

- Range validation: Verifies that numerical values fall within predefined ranges.

Consistency Validation:

- *Objective:* Ensures consistency within the dataset and across related datasets.
- *Techniques:*
  - Duplicate validation: Identifies and resolves duplicate records.
  - Referential integrity validation: Validates relationships between different datasets.

Business Rule Validation:

- *Objective:* Validates the adherence of data to specific business rules or criteria.
- *Techniques:*
  - Custom rule validation: Implements and validates against business-specific rules.
  - Compliance validation: Ensures data complies with regulatory or industry-specific standards.

2. Techniques for Data Validation:

Automated Validation Checks:

- *Implementation:* Employ automated scripts or tools to perform routine and repetitive validation checks.
- *Advantages:* Enhances efficiency and allows for regular validation as part of data processing workflows.

Statistical Validation:

- *Approach:* Utilize statistical methods to identify anomalies and deviations from expected patterns.

- *Techniques:* Mean, median, and standard deviation checks for numerical variables.

Data Profiling:

- *Methodology:* Create data profiles to summarize key statistics and characteristics of the dataset.

- *Application:* Identifies patterns, distributions, and potential issues for further validation.

Sampling Techniques:

- *Sampling Methods:* Random sampling or stratified sampling.

- *Purpose:* Validate a subset of data to infer the quality of the entire dataset.

3. Integration with Data Cleaning:

Iterative Validation and Cleaning:

- *Process:* Integrate validation checks into the data cleaning process.

- *Benefits:* Enhances the overall quality of the dataset by identifying and addressing issues iteratively.

Validation Documentation:

- *Documentation Practices:* Maintain a comprehensive record of validation procedures and outcomes.

- *Purpose:* Facilitates transparency, reproducibility, and collaboration among team members.

4. Practical Application:

Scenario:

Consider a healthcare dataset containing patient records, including medical diagnoses, treatments, and personal information.

Validation Techniques:

- Structural Validation: Ensure the dataset follows the predefined schema for patient records.
- Semantic Validation: Check for consistency in diagnoses and verify that treatments align with medical standards.
- Consistency Validation: Identify and resolve duplicate patient records for accurate reporting.
- Business Rule Validation: Validate compliance with healthcare regulations and standards.

Implementation:

- Utilize automated scripts to perform format validation for date of birth and other critical fields.
- Apply statistical validation to identify outliers in patient age distribution.
- Conduct cross-field validation to ensure coherence between diagnosis and prescribed treatments.

5. Challenges and Considerations:

Dynamic Data Environments:

- *Challenge:* Adapting validation techniques to dynamic datasets with evolving structures.

- *Consideration:* Establishing flexible validation procedures that accommodate changes.

Data Quality Metrics:

- *Challenge:* Defining and quantifying data quality metrics.
- *Consideration:* Regularly reassessing and updating metrics based on evolving data requirements.

6. Continuous Improvement:

Feedback Loop:

- *Establishment:* Create a feedback loop for ongoing validation improvements.
- *Benefits:* Enhances the effectiveness of validation techniques over time.

Conclusion:

Data validation techniques are the guardians of data integrity, ensuring that the foundation of analysis remains robust and trustworthy. By implementing a combination of structural, semantic, and consistency validation checks, analysts can confidently proceed with the assurance that their datasets meet high standards of accuracy and coherence. As we transition into the ethical considerations in data analysis, the integration of rigorous data validation practices lays the groundwork for responsible and reliable insights.

Step 1: Initial Assessment of the Dataset

Begin by conducting a thorough assessment of the dataset's structure, content, and adherence to predefined specifications. Identify key characteristics, potential challenges, and areas of focus for validation.

Step 2: Structural Validation

Objective: Ensure that the data structure conforms to predefined specifications.

Schema Validation:

- *Technique:* Use automated tools or scripts to verify that the dataset adheres to the predefined schema.

- *Example:* Check that each column corresponds to the expected data type and follows the specified naming conventions.

Format Validation:

- *Technique:* Implement format checks to confirm that data follows specified formats (e.g., date format, alphanumeric patterns).

- *Example:* Verify that dates are consistently formatted as YYYY-MM-DD.

Step 3: Semantic Validation

Objective: Validate the meaning and coherence of the data within and across datasets.

Cross-Field Validation:

- *Technique:* Check relationships between different fields to ensure consistency.

- *Example:* Validate that the gender field aligns with the title (Mr., Mrs., Ms.) field.

Range Validation:

- *Technique:* Verify that numerical values fall within predefined ranges.
- *Example:* Confirm that age values are within a reasonable range (e.g., 0 to 120 years).

Step 4: Consistency Validation

Objective: Ensure consistency within the dataset and across related datasets.

Duplicate Validation:

- *Technique:* Identify and resolve duplicate records based on key identifiers.
- *Example:* Identify and remove records with identical patient IDs and names.

Referential Integrity Validation:

- *Technique:* Validate relationships between different datasets (e.g., foreign key relationships).
- *Example:* Confirm that foreign keys in one dataset correspond to primary keys in another.

Step 5: Business Rule Validation

Objective: Validate the adherence of data to specific business rules or criteria.

Custom Rule Validation:

- *Technique:* Implement and validate against business-specific rules.
- *Example:* Ensure that sales data adheres to pricing and discount rules.

Compliance Validation:

- *Technique:* Ensure data complies with regulatory or industry-specific standards.

- *Example:* Validate that healthcare data adheres to privacy and security regulations.

Step 6: Automated Validation Checks

Implementation:

- *Technique:* Develop automated scripts or use tools to perform routine and repetitive validation checks.

- *Example:* Create a script to check for consistent formatting of phone numbers across the dataset.

Step 7: Statistical Validation

Approach: Utilize statistical methods to identify anomalies and deviations from expected patterns.

Techniques:

- *Mean, Median, Standard Deviation Checks:* Calculate and analyze key statistical measures for numerical variables.

- *Example:* Identify outliers in the distribution of test scores using standard deviation checks.

Step 8: Data Profiling

Methodology: Create data profiles to summarize key statistics and characteristics of the dataset.

Application:

- *Technique:* Generate summary statistics, histograms, and frequency distributions.
- *Example:* Create a data profile highlighting the distribution of customer ages.

Step 9: Sampling Techniques

Sampling Methods: Random sampling or stratified sampling.

Purpose: Validate a subset of data to infer the quality of the entire dataset.

Example:

- *Random Sampling:* Select a random sample of 100 records for detailed validation.
- *Stratified Sampling:* Validate data within specific strata (e.g., age groups).

Step 10: Integration with Data Cleaning

Iterative Validation and Cleaning:

- *Process:* Integrate validation checks into the data cleaning process.
- *Example:* Validate structural integrity after each data cleaning step.

Validation Documentation:

- *Documentation Practices:* Maintain detailed records of validation procedures and outcomes.

- *Example:* Document the results of each validation check, including any identified issues and resolutions.

Conclusion:

By following these step-by-step data validation techniques, analysts can ensure the integrity and reliability of their datasets. A systematic approach, combining structural, semantic, and consistency validation, sets the stage for ethical considerations in data analysis. As we transition to exploring ethical considerations, the foundation of robust data validation practices ensures that analytical insights are built on trustworthy and accurate data.

4.2 Ethical Considerations in Data Analysis

4.2.1 Privacy and Confidentiality

In the ever-expanding landscape of data analysis, ethical considerations play a pivotal role in safeguarding individual privacy and upholding the confidentiality of sensitive information. As data analysts delve into the realms of vast datasets, it becomes imperative to establish robust frameworks that prioritize privacy and confidentiality. This section explores the multifaceted dimensions of privacy and confidentiality, providing insights into best practices, legal considerations, and the ethical responsibilities that accompany the analysis of personal and confidential data.

1. Defining Privacy and Confidentiality in Data Analysis:

Privacy:

- *Definition:* The right of individuals to control the collection, use, and disclosure of their personal information.

- *Data Analysis Implications:* Ensuring that data analysts handle personal information with respect for individual rights and legal regulations.

Confidentiality:

- *Definition:* The obligation to protect sensitive information from unauthorized access or disclosure.

- *Data Analysis Implications:* Implementing measures to secure and restrict access to confidential data during analysis and dissemination.

2. Legal Frameworks and Compliance:

General Data Protection Regulation (GDPR):

- *Key Aspects:* Provides a comprehensive framework for protecting the privacy and rights of individuals.

- *Data Analysis Implications:* Data analysts must comply with GDPR regulations, including obtaining informed consent and ensuring data security.

Health Insurance Portability and Accountability Act (HIPAA):

- *Key Aspects:* Focuses on safeguarding the privacy and security of health-related information.

- *Data Analysis Implications:* Analysts working with health data must adhere to HIPAA guidelines and protocols.

Other Data Protection Laws:

- *Examples:* California Consumer Privacy Act (CCPA), Personal Information Protection and Electronic Documents Act (PIPEDA) in Canada.

- *Data Analysis Implications:* Awareness and adherence to regional data protection laws relevant to the dataset being analyzed.

3. Best Practices for Ensuring Privacy and Confidentiality:

Anonymization and Pseudonymization:

- *Strategy:* Replace or encrypt personally identifiable information (PII) to prevent direct identification.

- *Data Analysis Implications:* Implement anonymization techniques to minimize the risk of privacy breaches.

Secure Data Transmission:

- *Protocols:* Use secure channels such as HTTPS for transmitting sensitive data.

- *Data Analysis Implications:* Safeguarding data during transmission prevents interception by unauthorized entities.

Role-Based Access Control (RBAC):

- *Implementation:* Restrict access to sensitive data based on individuals' roles and responsibilities.

- *Data Analysis Implications:* Ensuring that only authorized personnel have access to confidential datasets.

Informed Consent:

- *Procedure:* Obtain explicit consent from individuals before collecting and using their data.

- *Data Analysis Implications:* Prioritize transparency and ensure that individuals understand how their data will be used.

Data Encryption:

- *Technology:* Implement encryption algorithms to protect data at rest.

- *Data Analysis Implications:* Safeguarding data integrity and confidentiality throughout the analysis process.

4. Ethical Responsibilities of Data Analysts:

Transparent Communication:

- *Practice:* Clearly communicate the purpose and scope of data analysis to stakeholders.

- *Data Analysis Implications:* Foster trust by keeping stakeholders informed about how their data will be used.

Responsible Handling of Bias:

- *Approach:* Identify and mitigate bias in data collection and analysis.

- *Data Analysis Implications:* Acknowledge and address biases to prevent unfair or discriminatory outcomes.

Continuous Education and Awareness:

- *Initiatives:* Stay informed about evolving privacy regulations and ethical standards.

- *Data Analysis Implications:* Regular training and awareness programs for data analysts to uphold ethical practices.

5. Case Studies: Balancing Analysis and Privacy Protection:

Healthcare Analytics:

- *Scenario:* Analyzing patient data to improve healthcare outcomes.

- *Data Analysis Implications:* Strict adherence to HIPAA regulations, de-identification of patient information, and secure data transmission.

Marketing Analytics:

- *Scenario:* Utilizing consumer data for targeted marketing strategies.

- *Data Analysis Implications:* Compliance with GDPR and CCPA, obtaining explicit consent, and ensuring transparent communication with consumers.

6. Challenges and Mitigations:

Emerging Technologies:

- *Challenge:* Addressing ethical concerns posed by emerging technologies like facial recognition.

- *Mitigation:* Engaging in public discourse, establishing industry standards, and advocating for responsible use.

Big Data and Algorithmic Bias:

- *Challenge:* Mitigating biases in algorithms when analyzing vast datasets.

- *Mitigation:* Implementing fairness-enhancing techniques, regular audits, and involving diverse perspectives in algorithm development.

7. Future Trends and Considerations:

Ethics in AI:

- *Consideration:* Integrating ethical considerations into the development and deployment of AI algorithms.

- *Data Analysis Implications:* Adopting ethical AI frameworks and principles to guide data analysis practices.

Global Collaboration on Privacy Standards:

- *Consideration:* Collaborating across borders to establish consistent global privacy standards.

- *Data Analysis Implications:* Navigating diverse legal landscapes and adhering to the highest privacy standards.

8. Conclusion: Balancing Insightful Analysis and Ethical Principles:

In the intricate dance between extracting valuable insights and upholding ethical principles, data analysts play a critical role. Balancing the pursuit of knowledge with the responsibility to protect privacy and confidentiality requires a nuanced understanding of legal frameworks, best practices, and continuous ethical reflection. As data analysis continues to evolve, a commitment to ethical considerations becomes not only a professional obligation but a cornerstone for building a trustworthy and responsible data-driven society.

4.2.2 Responsible Data Use

In the era of unprecedented data availability and technological advancements, the ethical use of data is of paramount importance. Responsible data use goes beyond compliance with legal frameworks; it involves a conscientious approach to handling, analyzing, and disseminating data to ensure positive impacts on individuals, communities, and society as a whole. This section explores the principles and practices associated with responsible data use, shedding light on the ethical responsibilities that data analysts bear in their pursuit of insights.

1. Defining Responsible Data Use:

Holistic Perspective:

- *Definition:* Responsible data use encompasses the ethical, social, and environmental considerations associated with the entire data lifecycle.

- *Data Analysis Implications:* Data analysts should approach their work with a comprehensive understanding of the potential consequences and benefits of their actions.

Impact on Stakeholders:

- *Definition:* Assessing how data analysis activities may impact individuals, communities, and organizations.

- *Data Analysis Implications:* Acknowledging the diverse stakeholders involved and considering their perspectives in decision-making.

2. Key Principles of Responsible Data Use:

Transparency:

- *Principle:* Communicate openly about data collection, analysis methods, and the intended use of insights.

- *Implementation:* Clearly document and communicate the purpose, methods, and potential impacts of data analysis to stakeholders.

Fairness and Equity:

- *Principle:* Ensure that data analysis processes and outcomes do not perpetuate or exacerbate existing inequalities.

- *Implementation:* Regularly assess and mitigate bias in algorithms and data sources to promote fairness.

Informed Consent:

- *Principle:* Obtain explicit consent from individuals before using their data for analysis.

- *Implementation:* Establish clear and accessible consent mechanisms, providing individuals with information about how their data will be used.

Data Minimization:

- *Principle:* Collect and use only the data necessary for the intended analysis, minimizing unnecessary intrusion.

- *Implementation:* Conduct thorough assessments to determine the minimum dataset required for analysis, avoiding data over-collection.

Data Security:

- *Principle:* Safeguard data against unauthorized access, disclosure, or misuse.

- *Implementation:* Implement robust encryption, access controls, and secure data transmission protocols to protect sensitive information.

3. Balancing Innovation and Ethical Considerations:

Emerging Technologies:

- *Consideration:* Evaluating the ethical implications of adopting emerging technologies in data analysis.

- *Data Analysis Implications:* Balancing innovation with ethical considerations to ensure responsible use of cutting-edge tools and techniques.

Ethical AI and Machine Learning:

- *Consideration:* Integrating ethical considerations into the development and deployment of AI and machine learning models.

- *Data Analysis Implications:* Adhering to ethical AI principles, conducting impact assessments, and addressing biases in algorithms.

4. Responsible Data Use in Practice:

Healthcare Analytics:

- *Scenario:* Analyzing patient data to improve treatment outcomes.

- *Data Analysis Implications:* Prioritizing patient privacy, obtaining informed consent, and ensuring that insights contribute positively to patient care.

Financial Services Analytics:

- *Scenario:* Utilizing customer data for credit scoring.

- *Data Analysis Implications:* Adhering to fair lending practices, ensuring transparency in credit scoring algorithms, and mitigating biases.

5. Continuous Monitoring and Evaluation:

Ethical Audits:

- *Practice:* Conducting regular ethical audits to assess the impact of data analysis activities.

- *Data Analysis Implications:* Identifying and addressing ethical concerns proactively through systematic evaluations.

Feedback Mechanisms:

- *Practice:* Establishing mechanisms for stakeholders to provide feedback on data use practices.

- *Data Analysis Implications:* Incorporating stakeholder feedback to improve ethical practices and responsiveness to concerns.

6. Challenges and Mitigations:

Data Governance:

- *Challenge:* Ensuring consistent ethical standards across diverse datasets and contexts.

- *Mitigation:* Establishing robust data governance frameworks that prioritize ethical considerations and compliance.

Navigating Legal and Ethical Boundaries:

- *Challenge:* Balancing legal requirements with ethical considerations in data use.

- *Mitigation:* Seeking legal guidance, engaging in ethical discourse, and advocating for ethical practices within organizational frameworks.

7. Future Trends and Considerations:

Ethics in AI Research:

- *Consideration:* Integrating ethical considerations into AI research methodologies.

- *Data Analysis Implications:* Ensuring responsible practices in AI research, including transparent reporting and minimizing unintended consequences.

Public Discourse on Responsible Data Use:

- *Consideration:* Fostering open discussions about responsible data use in the public domain.

- *Data Analysis Implications:* Engaging in transparent communication with the public, addressing concerns, and incorporating public perspectives in ethical decision-making.

8. Conclusion: Striking the Balance Between Innovation and Responsibility:

In the dynamic landscape of data analysis, responsible data use emerges as a guiding principle for ethical decision-making. By embracing transparency, fairness, and continuous evaluation, data analysts can contribute to a culture of ethical responsibility that aligns with the evolving expectations of society. As technology advances, ethical considerations must remain at the forefront, guiding data analysts towards innovations that not only push the boundaries of knowledge but also uphold the values of fairness, equity, and respect for individual privacy.

CHAPTER V
Communicating Results Effectively

5.1 Data Visualization Best Practices

5.1.1 Choosing the Right Visualization

In the realm of data analysis, the ability to convey insights through effective visualizations is paramount. Choosing the right visualization method is a critical step that influences how information is perceived, understood, and acted upon. This section explores the principles and considerations behind selecting the appropriate visualization techniques, offering insights into the types of data and scenarios where specific visualizations excel.

1. Understanding Data Types and Visualization Techniques:

Nominal Data:

- *Definition:* Categorical data without inherent order.
- *Appropriate Visualizations:*
  - *Bar Charts:* Displaying frequency distribution.
  - *Pie Charts:* Illustrating the proportion of categories in a whole.

Ordinal Data:

- *Definition:* Categorical data with a meaningful order.
- *Appropriate Visualizations:*
  - *Bar Charts:* Showing rank or order.
  - *Dot Plots:* Representing order without emphasizing magnitude.

Interval Data:

- *Definition:* Numerical data with equal intervals between values but no true zero point.
- *Appropriate Visualizations:*
  - *Histograms:* Visualizing distribution and frequency.
  - *Line Charts:* Displaying trends over time.

Ratio Data:

- *Definition:* Numerical data with equal intervals and a true zero point.
- *Appropriate Visualizations:*
  - *Scatter Plots:* Showing relationships and correlations.
  - *Box Plots:* Highlighting distribution characteristics.

2. Matching Visualization to Analysis Goals:

Comparison:

- *Goal:* Highlighting differences between values.
- *Visualizations:*
  - *Bar Charts:* Comparing quantities across categories.
  - *Line Charts:* Contrasting trends over time.

Distribution:

- *Goal:* Understanding the spread and frequency of values.
- *Visualizations:*
  - *Histograms:* Displaying frequency distributions.
  - *Box Plots:* Illustrating central tendency and variability.

Relationships:

- *Goal:* Identifying correlations and patterns.
- *Visualizations:*
  - *Scatter Plots:* Visualizing the relationship between two variables.
  - *Correlation Heatmaps:* Displaying correlation matrices.

3. Tailoring Visualizations to Audience:

Executive Summary:

- *Audience:* Senior executives and decision-makers.
- *Visualizations:*
  - *Dashboard Summaries:* Providing high-level overviews.
  - *Infographics:* Presenting key insights visually.

Technical Audience:

- *Audience:* Data scientists and analysts.
- *Visualizations:*

- *Advanced Charts:* Including detailed visualizations with statistical details.
- *Custom Plots:* Catering to the technical expertise of the audience.

4. Avoiding Common Pitfalls in Visualization Selection:

Misleading Representations:

- *Pitfall:* Choosing visualizations that distort the true nature of the data.
- *Prevention:* Prioritize accuracy and clarity over flashy or misleading visuals.

Overcomplication:

- *Pitfall:* Creating overly complex visualizations that confuse the audience.
- *Prevention:* Simplify visuals to convey the message clearly without unnecessary complexity.

5. Utilizing Interactive Features:

Interactivity:

- *Advantage:* Allowing users to explore and interact with the data.
- *Examples:*
  - *Interactive Dashboards:* Enabling users to customize their view.
  - *Drill-Down Functionality:* Providing detailed information on demand.

6. Case Studies: Real-World Applications of Visualization Choices:

Financial Performance Analysis:

- *Scenario:* Presenting quarterly financial performance to stakeholders.

- *Visualization Choices:* Bar charts for comparing revenue, line charts for trends, and a dashboard for an overview.

Customer Segmentation:

- *Scenario:* Analyzing customer demographics and preferences.

- *Visualization Choices:* Pie charts for demographic proportions, scatter plots for correlations, and an interactive dashboard for exploration.

7. Tools and Platforms for Effective Visualization:

Data Visualization Tools:

- *Examples:* Tableau, Power BI, matplotlib (Python).

- *Considerations:* Choosing tools based on ease of use, customization options, and compatibility with data sources.

8. Future Trends in Data Visualization:

Augmented Reality (AR) and Virtual Reality (VR):

- *Trend:* Integrating AR and VR for immersive data exploration.

- *Implications:* Enhancing user engagement and providing innovative ways to interact with data.

Explainable AI Visualizations:

- *Trend:* Visualizing AI model outputs to enhance interpretability.

- *Implications:* Building trust in AI-driven insights through transparent visual representations.

9. Best Practices and Takeaways:

Iterative Design Process:

- *Practice:* Iteratively refine visualizations based on feedback.
- *Takeaway:* Continuous improvement leads to more effective communication.

Feedback and Collaboration:

- *Practice:* Solicit feedback from diverse stakeholders.
- *Takeaway:* Collaborative efforts lead to visualizations that resonate with the intended audience.

10. Conclusion: Choosing Wisely for Impactful Communication:

In the dynamic landscape of data visualization, the ability to choose the right visualization method is an art and a science. By aligning visualization choices with analysis goals, audience preferences, and data characteristics, analysts can elevate their communication impact. As technology evolves and new trends emerge, the key remains in making informed decisions that transform data into meaningful, actionable insights through the judicious selection of visualizations.

Certainly! Let's consider a scenario where a data analyst is tasked with presenting sales performance data for a retail company over the past year. The goal is to communicate key insights to both the executive team and the sales department. In this context, we'll explore how the data analyst might choose the right visualizations for different aspects of the analysis.

1. Comparison of Quarterly Sales:

Data Type: Numerical (Ratio Data - Sales Revenue)

Goal: Highlighting differences in sales revenue across quarters.

Chosen Visualization: Bar Charts

Explanation: Bar charts are effective for comparing quantities across categories, making them suitable for displaying the sales revenue for each quarter. Each bar represents a quarter, allowing stakeholders to easily compare performance visually.

2. Trends in Monthly Sales:

Data Type: Numerical (Interval Data - Monthly Sales)

Goal: Showing trends and patterns in monthly sales.

Chosen Visualization: Line Chart

Explanation: A line chart is suitable for illustrating trends over time. Each point on the line represents the sales for a specific month, allowing the audience to identify patterns, seasonality, and overall trends in sales performance.

3. Customer Segmentation:

Data Type: Categorical (Nominal Data - Customer Segments)

Goal: Analyzing the distribution of sales among different customer segments.

Chosen Visualization: Pie Chart

Explanation: Pie charts are effective for showcasing proportions of a whole. In this case, a pie chart can represent the distribution of sales among different customer segments, providing a quick visual overview of the contribution of each segment to the total sales.

4. Correlation Between Marketing Expenses and Sales:

Data Type: Numerical (Ratio Data - Sales Revenue, Marketing Expenses)

Goal: Identifying the relationship between marketing expenses and sales revenue.

Chosen Visualization: Scatter Plot

Explanation: Scatter plots are ideal for visualizing relationships between two numerical variables. Each point on the plot represents a combination of marketing expenses and sales revenue, allowing stakeholders to observe patterns and correlations.

5. Interactive Dashboard for Overall Performance:

Data Type: Multiple (Various KPIs - Sales, Expenses, Profit)

Goal: Providing an interactive overview of overall performance.

Chosen Visualization: Interactive Dashboard

Explanation: An interactive dashboard combines multiple visualizations, such as bar charts, line charts, and key performance indicators (KPIs), into a single interface. Users can customize their view, drill down into specific details, and gain a comprehensive understanding of overall performance.

This example demonstrates how the choice of visualizations depends on the nature of the data, the goals of the analysis, and the preferences of the audience. By carefully selecting and combining visualizations, the data analyst can effectively communicate insights, enabling stakeholders to make informed decisions based on the presented data.

5.1.2 Design Principles for Effective Visuals

The effectiveness of data visualizations extends beyond the choice of chart types; it heavily relies on the design principles applied to convey information clearly and facilitate understanding. In this section, we delve into the essential design principles that enhance the clarity, aesthetics, and impact of data visuals.

1. Clarity and Simplicity:

Clear Communication:

- *Principle:* Prioritize clear communication of insights.

- *Implementation:* Eliminate unnecessary elements, labels, or decorations that may distract from the main message.

Simplicity in Design:

- *Principle:* Embrace simplicity in visual elements.
- *Implementation:* Use clean and straightforward design elements to avoid overwhelming the audience.

2. Consistency in Design Elements:

Color Consistency:

- *Principle:* Maintain consistency in color usage.
- *Implementation:* Choose a cohesive color palette and stick to it across all visualizations for a unified look.

Font and Text Consistency:

- *Principle:* Ensure uniformity in font styles and text size.
- *Implementation:* Use a consistent font type and size for titles, labels, and annotations.

3. Effective Use of Color:

Color Meaning:

- *Principle:* Leverage color to convey meaning.
- *Implementation:* Assign distinct colors to different categories or data points to aid interpretation.

Avoiding Overuse:

- *Principle:* Avoid overusing colors that may distract.

- *Implementation:* Limit the color palette to essential elements, preventing visual clutter.

4. Proper Use of Text and Annotations:

Informative Labels:

- *Principle:* Ensure labels provide meaningful information.

- *Implementation:* Clearly label data points, axes, and other elements to guide interpretation.

Strategic Annotations:

- *Principle:* Use annotations strategically for emphasis.

- *Implementation:* Add annotations to highlight key insights or trends, providing context to the audience.

5. Visualization Layout and Spacing:

Optimal Layout:

- *Principle:* Design layouts for optimal information absorption.

- *Implementation:* Arrange visual elements logically, considering the flow of information.

Adequate Spacing:

- *Principle:* Maintain sufficient spacing between elements.

- *Implementation:* Prevent overcrowding by providing ample space between charts, labels, and annotations.

6. Accessibility and Inclusivity:

Contrast for Accessibility:

- *Principle:* Prioritize contrast for accessibility.

- *Implementation:* Ensure sufficient contrast between text and background to accommodate individuals with visual impairments.

Consideration for Color Blindness:

- *Principle:* Design with color blindness in mind.

- *Implementation:* Use patterns, labels, or distinctive markers in addition to color to convey information.

7. Engaging Visual Hierarchy:

Hierarchy of Information:

- *Principle:* Establish a clear visual hierarchy.

- *Implementation:* Emphasize critical information through size, color, or positioning to guide the audience's attention.

Focal Points:

- *Principle:* Create focal points for key insights.

- *Implementation:* Designate specific elements or visualizations as focal points to draw attention to essential findings.

8. Responsiveness for Various Platforms:

Adaptability:

- *Principle:* Design visuals for adaptability across devices.

- *Implementation:* Ensure that visualizations are responsive and maintain clarity on various platforms, including desktops, tablets, and mobile devices.

9. Iterative Design and Feedback:

Continuous Improvement:

- *Principle:* Embrace iterative design for continuous improvement.

- *Implementation:* Solicit feedback from stakeholders, iterate on designs, and refine visuals based on input.

10. Case Studies: Applying Design Principles in Real-world Scenarios:

Financial Report Visualization:

- *Scenario:* Designing a financial report for executive review.

- *Design Principles:* Clarity, simplicity, color meaning, and hierarchy to highlight key financial metrics.

Sales Dashboard for Marketing Team:

- *Scenario:* Creating a sales dashboard for the marketing team.

- *Design Principles:* Consistency, effective use of color, and responsive design for accessibility across devices.

11. Tools and Platforms for Designing Effective Visuals:

Data Visualization Software:

- *Examples:* Tableau, Power BI, D3.js.

- *Considerations:* Choose tools with features that facilitate adherence to design principles.

12. Future Trends in Data Visualization Design:

Augmented Reality (AR) Integration:

- *Trend:* Integrating AR for immersive data visualization experiences.

- *Implications:* Enhancing user engagement and interaction with data in three-dimensional spaces.

Automated Design Assistance:

- *Trend:* Implementation of AI-driven tools for automated design suggestions.

- *Implications: Streamlining* the design process and ensuring adherence to best practices.

13. Conclusion: Elevating Impact Through Thoughtful Design:

In the realm of data visualization, the marriage of insightful content and effective design principles is paramount. By adopting principles of clarity, consistency, and inclusivity, data analysts can craft visuals that not only convey information but also resonate with and engage their audience. As technology evolves and new design trends emerge, the timeless principles outlined in this chapter remain foundational for creating visuals that leave a lasting impact.

5.2 Building Data Dashboards

5.2.1 Selecting Dashboard Components

Data dashboards serve as powerful tools for presenting complex information in a visually accessible manner. The effectiveness of a dashboard heavily relies on the careful selection of components tailored to the specific needs of the audience and objectives. In this section, we delve into the key considerations and best practices for selecting dashboard components.

 # 1. Understanding Dashboard Components

Before diving into the selection process, it's crucial to have a clear understanding of the available dashboard components. These can include:

1.1 Metrics and KPIs

Metrics and Key Performance Indicators (KPIs) are fundamental elements providing a quick overview of performance. Carefully choose those directly aligned with the goals of your analysis or the needs of your stakeholders.

1.2 Charts and Graphs

Different visualizations convey data in distinct ways. Select charts and graphs that effectively communicate your message. Consider bar charts for comparisons, line charts for trends, and pie charts for proportional data.

1.3 Tables

Tables offer a detailed, structured view of numerical data. Use them judiciously to present specific values or allow users to explore detailed information.

1.4 Maps

For geospatial data, maps can be indispensable. They provide a geographical context to the data and help identify patterns or trends across different regions.

1.5 Filters and Interactivity

Allow users to interact with the data by incorporating filters. Dynamic elements enhance the user experience, enabling them to focus on specific subsets or time frames.

1.6 Text and Annotations

Incorporate textual elements to provide context, explanations, or call attention to important findings. Annotations can guide users through the dashboard and highlight key insights.

2. Aligning Components with Objectives

2.1 Audience-Centric Approach

Consider the preferences and familiarity of your target audience. Components that resonate with stakeholders and decision-makers will enhance engagement and understanding.

2.2 Information Hierarchy

Establish a clear hierarchy of information. Prioritize the most critical components to ensure that users grasp essential insights quickly. Arrange components logically to guide the viewer's attention.

2.3 Balancing Detail and Simplicity

Strike a balance between providing detailed information and maintaining simplicity. Avoid overwhelming the dashboard with excessive components, focusing on clarity and conciseness.

3. Best Practices in Component Selection

3.1 Consistency in Design

Maintain a consistent design language across all components for a cohesive and professional appearance. Consistency fosters familiarity and ease of use.

3.2 Responsiveness

Ensure that the selected components are responsive to different screen sizes and devices. A well-designed dashboard adapts seamlessly to varying display environments.

3.3 Scalability

Consider the scalability of the components concerning future data additions or modifications. A scalable dashboard accommodates evolving analytical needs.

4. Iterative Refinement

Dashboard development is an iterative process. Gather feedback from users and stakeholders, and be prepared to refine component selection based on evolving requirements and insights gained through usage.

Conclusion

Selecting the right dashboard components is an art that combines an understanding of data visualization principles, user needs, and communication objectives. By following these considerations and best practices, you can create a compelling and effective dashboard that resonates with your audience, facilitating informed decision-making and insights extraction.

Example Illustration:

To better understand the principles discussed in selecting dashboard components, let's consider a scenario where we are tasked with creating a data dashboard for a retail company analyzing sales performance over time.

1. Metrics and KPIs:

- Selected Key Performance Indicators (KPIs): Total Revenue, Average Transaction Value, and Customer Acquisition Cost.

- Metrics: Monthly Sales Growth Rate and Year-to-Date Sales.

2. Charts and Graphs:

- Bar Chart: Monthly sales comparisons for the past year.

- Line Chart: Trends in the Average Transaction Value over quarters.

- Pie Chart: Proportional breakdown of revenue by product category.

3. Tables:

- Tabular display of detailed sales data, including product-level information, salesperson performance, and customer demographics.

4. Maps:

- Geospatial map illustrating sales distribution across different regions, helping identify areas with high and low sales performance.

5. Filters and Interactivity:

- Time filter allowing users to focus on specific quarters or months.

- Product category filter for users interested in a particular product segment.

- Interactive tooltips providing detailed information on-demand.

6. Text and Annotations:

- Textual insights summarizing key findings and actionable recommendations.

- Annotations highlighting exceptional months or identifying significant changes in sales patterns.

Alignment with Objectives:

- **Audience-Centric Approach:** Considering that stakeholders include both executives and sales managers, the dashboard aims to provide a balance of high-level insights and detailed information catering to different user preferences.

- **Information Hierarchy:** Prioritizing KPIs at the top, followed by visualizations and detailed tables, ensuring a logical flow of information for quick comprehension.

- **Balancing Detail and Simplicity:** Avoiding information overload by displaying the most relevant data, using tooltips for additional details, and maintaining a clean design.

Best Practices in Component Selection:

- **Consistency in Design:** Ensuring a uniform color scheme, font, and style throughout the dashboard for a cohesive appearance.

- **Responsiveness:** Testing the dashboard on various devices to guarantee a seamless user experience, whether accessed on desktops, tablets, or smartphones.

- **Scalability:** Designing the dashboard components to accommodate potential additions of new product lines or regions in the future.

Iterative Refinement:

- Gathering feedback through usability testing and stakeholder reviews.

- Being open to adjusting the dashboard components based on user suggestions or evolving business requirements.

By applying these principles and components to the retail sales analysis scenario, we create a dynamic and user-friendly dashboard that effectively communicates insights, aiding decision-makers in understanding and acting upon the presented data.

5.2.2 Creating Interactive Dashboards

In the era of data-driven decision-making, static dashboards fall short of meeting the evolving needs of users who seek more than just visual representations of data—they desire engagement and interactivity. This section explores the art and science of creating interactive dashboards, focusing on the tools, techniques, and best practices that elevate data exploration and analysis.

 # 1. The Power of Interactivity

Interactive dashboards empower users to move beyond passive observation, allowing them to actively engage with the data. The benefits are manifold:

1.1 User Engagement:

Interactivity enhances user engagement by enabling exploration, customization, and a sense of control over the presented information.

1.2 Dynamic Insights:

Users can derive dynamic insights by adjusting parameters, applying filters, and drilling down into specific data subsets.

1.3 Real-time Decision Support:

The ability to interact with real-time data facilitates quicker and more informed decision-making.

2. Tools for Creating Interactive Dashboards

2.1 Business Intelligence (BI) Platforms:

BI tools like Tableau, Power BI, and Qlik provide user-friendly interfaces for building interactive dashboards. They offer drag-and-drop functionality, a variety of visualization options, and support for data connections.

2.2 JavaScript Libraries:

For those with coding expertise, JavaScript libraries such as D3.js and Plotly.js offer extensive customization options, allowing the creation of highly interactive and personalized dashboards.

2.3 Excel and Google Sheets:

Even spreadsheet tools like Excel and Google Sheets provide features for creating basic interactive dashboards through slicers, pivot tables, and dynamic charts.

3. Designing Interactive Elements

3.1 Filters and Dropdowns:

Implementing filters allows users to selectively view data based on specified criteria. Dropdown menus enhance user experience by providing a structured way to interact with the dashboard.

3.2 Clickable Elements:

Integrate clickable elements such as buttons or icons to trigger specific actions, such as navigating to another dashboard, opening additional information, or resetting filters.

3.3 Interactive Charts:

Choose visualizations that respond to user interactions, allowing for dynamic exploration. For instance, users can click on a data point in a chart to see more detailed information or to cross-filter other components.

4. Best Practices in Interactive Dashboard Creation

4.1 Performance Optimization:

Optimize dashboard performance to ensure responsiveness, especially when dealing with large datasets. Implement lazy loading or data aggregation techniques to enhance speed.

4.2 User Guidance:

Provide tooltips, hints, or a user guide to help users understand the interactive features and make the most of the dashboard's capabilities.

4.3 Accessibility:

Ensure that the dashboard remains accessible to users with varying levels of technical expertise. Design features with simplicity and clarity in mind.

 # 5. Creating a Seamless User Experience

5.1 Story Flow:

Design the dashboard with a logical flow, guiding users through a narrative or analytical journey. Each interaction should contribute to a cohesive user experience.

5.2 Responsive Design:

Ensure the dashboard is responsive across different devices, adapting its layout and interactivity to various screen sizes.

 # 6. Iterative Development and Testing

6.1 User Feedback:

Encourage user feedback during the development phase and iterate based on user suggestions to enhance usability.

6.2 Cross-browser Compatibility:

Test the dashboard across different web browsers to guarantee a consistent and functional experience for all users.

 # 7. Case Study: Dynamic Sales Dashboard

To illustrate the principles discussed, consider a dynamic sales dashboard created with Tableau. Users can interactively explore sales performance by adjusting time filters, selecting specific product categories, and clicking on data points to reveal detailed information.

In conclusion, creating interactive dashboards requires a thoughtful blend of design, technology, and user-centric considerations. By leveraging the right tools and adhering to best practices, analysts and data professionals can deliver a rich and engaging experience, empowering users to unlock valuable insights from their data.

Illustrative Example: Dynamic Sales Dashboard

Let's walk through an example of creating a dynamic sales dashboard using Tableau, showcasing how interactivity can enhance the user experience and provide valuable insights.

 # Dashboard Components:

1. Main Overview:

- Displaying total revenue, sales trends, and key performance indicators.

- Interactive time filter (dropdown or slider) allowing users to adjust the date range dynamically.

2. Product Sales Breakdown:

- Stacked bar chart illustrating sales distribution by product category.

- Clickable segments for each category, triggering a cross-filter effect on other components.

3. Regional Performance Map:

- Geospatial map showing sales data across different regions.

- Color-coded markers indicating sales intensity, with an interactive legend for clarity.

- Clickable regions to filter other components based on the selected area.

4. Salesperson Contribution:

- Table listing top-performing salespersons.

- Clickable names for individual salespersons, updating other components to reflect their specific contributions.

5. Dynamic Insights Panel:

- Textual insights dynamically updating based on user interactions.

- Providing context and highlighting notable trends or anomalies.

 # Interactivity Scenarios:

1. Time Exploration:

- User adjusts the time filter to focus on a specific quarter, instantly updating all charts and tables accordingly.

2. Product Analysis:

- Clicking on a product category in the bar chart filters the regional map and salesperson table to show data related to that specific category.

3. Regional Drill-Down:

- Clicking on a region in the map filters all other components to display information specific to that region, providing a localized view.

4. Salesperson Deep Dive:

- Selecting a salesperson's name in the table updates the entire dashboard to showcase their individual performance metrics.

 # User Guidance and Accessibility:

- Tooltips and Instructions:

- Providing tooltips for each interactive element to guide users on how to use the features effectively.

- Including a brief onboarding guide or tutorial for new users.

- Simplicity in Design:

- Ensuring that the dashboard layout remains clean and intuitive, minimizing complexity for users of varying technical backgrounds.

 # Responsive Design:

- Adapting to Different Devices:

- Testing the dashboard on desktops, tablets, and smartphones to ensure a seamless experience across all devices.

 # Iterative Development:

- User Feedback Loop:

- Encouraging users to provide feedback during beta testing to identify any usability issues or areas for improvement.

- Iterating the dashboard based on user suggestions to enhance overall usability.

 # Conclusion:

By integrating these interactive features into the sales dashboard, users gain the flexibility to explore and analyze data dynamically. This not only enhances their understanding of sales performance but also facilitates quicker and more informed decision-making. The example demonstrates the practical application of creating an interactive dashboard that goes beyond static representations, offering a dynamic and engaging user experience.

5.3 Telling a Compelling Data Story

5.3.1 Structuring Your Narrative

Effective data analysis is not just about numbers and charts; it's about telling a compelling story that resonates with your audience. In this section, we explore the art of structuring a narrative within the context of data analysis. Crafting a narrative around your findings not only enhances understanding but also makes the data more memorable and actionable for stakeholders.

 # 1. Understanding the Power of Narrative in Data Analysis

1.1 Contextualizing Data:

- Start by setting the stage. Provide context for the analysis, outlining the problem or question at hand. This helps orient stakeholders and creates a foundation for the narrative.

1.2 Humanizing Data:

- Make the data relatable by connecting it to real-world scenarios or specific challenges faced by the organization. Humanizing data adds a layer of empathy, making it more impactful.

1.3 Framing the Story:

- Define the central theme of your narrative. What overarching message or insight do you want your audience to take away? This theme serves as the guiding thread throughout your story.

 # 2. Elements of a Data Narrative

2.1 Introduction:

- Introduce the dataset and its significance to the organization. Clearly state the purpose of the analysis and the specific questions you aim to answer.

2.2 Plot Development:

- Build the narrative progressively. Present data points and insights in a logical sequence, allowing stakeholders to follow the flow of your analysis effortlessly.

2.3 Conflict and Resolution:

- Identify key challenges or anomalies in the data as the 'conflict.' Then, provide resolutions or actionable insights as the 'resolution.' This structure creates a sense of progression and resolution for the audience.

2.4 Character Development (If Applicable):

- If your analysis involves different segments, products, or departments, treat them as characters in your story. Develop their 'story arcs' to add depth to the narrative.

2.5 Visual Storytelling:

- Integrate visuals strategically. Charts, graphs, and images should complement the narrative, enhancing understanding and reinforcing key points.

3. Tailoring Your Narrative to the Audience

3.1 Stakeholder-Centric Approach:

- Consider the background, interests, and priorities of your audience. Tailor the narrative to resonate with their perspectives and address their specific concerns.

3.2 Balancing Detail:

- Strike a balance between providing sufficient detail for a comprehensive understanding and avoiding overwhelming stakeholders with technical intricacies. Cater to both experts and non-experts in your audience.

4. Techniques for Narrative Structuring

4.1 Chronological Order:

- Presenting data in chronological order can be effective for showcasing trends, changes, or the evolution of a situation over time.

4.2 Problem-Solution Framework:

- Frame your narrative around identified problems and provide data-supported solutions. This approach aligns with decision-making and action-oriented perspectives.

4.3 Comparative Analysis:

- Use comparative analysis to highlight contrasts and similarities, aiding stakeholders in understanding variations across different segments or time periods.

5. Engaging Your Audience

5.1 Story Arcs and Climaxes:

- Structure your narrative like a story with arcs and climaxes. Build tension by introducing challenges and release it by presenting insightful resolutions.

5.2 Interactive Storytelling (If Applicable):

- If using an interactive dashboard, incorporate elements that allow stakeholders to explore the narrative at their own pace. This can include clickable insights, drill-down features, or scenario-based analyses.

6. Iterative Refinement

6.1 Feedback Loops:

- Seek feedback on your narrative from stakeholders. Understand their perspectives and refine the storytelling elements based on their input.

6.2 Continuous Improvement:

- Treat narrative creation as an iterative process. As new data becomes available or business goals evolve, update and enhance your narrative to maintain relevance.

7. Case Study: Sales Performance Analysis

To illustrate the principles discussed, consider a case study where a data analyst presents a narrative on sales performance, addressing challenges, showcasing growth opportunities, and proposing strategic actions. The narrative incorporates a well-structured plot, visual elements, and tailors the story to resonate with both sales teams and executive leadership.

Conclusion: Crafting Impactful Data Stories

In conclusion, structuring a narrative around data is an essential skill in the data analyst's toolkit. It transforms raw information into a compelling story that not only informs but also inspires action. By understanding the elements of a good narrative, tailoring it to the audience, and embracing iterative refinement, data analysts can elevate their communication skills and make data-driven insights more accessible and influential.

Illustrative Example: Sales Performance Analysis Narrative

Introduction:

Imagine you're a data analyst tasked with presenting a comprehensive analysis of the company's sales performance over the past year. The goal is to provide actionable insights to the sales team and executive leadership. Let's structure a narrative around this scenario.

1. Contextualizing Data:

- Start by introducing the dataset: "In the ever-evolving landscape of our industry, understanding our sales performance is crucial for staying competitive. Over the past year, we've collected data on product sales, customer behavior, and market trends."

2. Humanizing Data:

- Connect the data to real-world scenarios: "Consider the challenges our sales team faced — adapting to market shifts, responding to customer feedback, and navigating the impacts of global events. Our data holds the story of their efforts."

3. Framing the Story:

- Define the central theme: "This analysis aims to uncover the drivers of our sales performance, identify areas of opportunity, and propose strategic actions for continued growth."

Plot Development:

4. Introduction of Challenges:

- "As we delve into the data, we encounter challenges. Despite a steady increase in leads, conversion rates have plateaued. This 'conflict' becomes the focal point of our narrative."

5. Trends and Patterns:

- "Plot development involves revealing data trends: certain products consistently outperforming others, regional variations, and the impact of marketing campaigns on customer engagement."

6. Conflict and Resolution:

- "The conflict arises as we identify bottlenecks in the sales funnel, hindering conversion. The resolution lies in optimizing the customer journey, streamlining processes, and leveraging successful product lines to enhance overall performance."

Visual Storytelling:

7. Interactive Charts:

- "Let's interactively explore our sales map. Click on regions to see detailed performance metrics. This visual storytelling technique engages stakeholders in understanding geographical sales dynamics."

8. Dynamic Insights Panel:

- "As we move through the narrative, an insights panel dynamically updates, providing instant takeaways. For instance, clicking on a specific product category reveals its contribution to overall revenue."

Tailoring to the Audience:

9. Sales Team Focus:

- "For our sales team: Here are actionable insights to enhance your efforts. Identify high-performing products, prioritize regions with untapped potential, and leverage customer feedback to refine your approach."

10. Executive Leadership Perspective:

- "For our executives: This narrative outlines strategic initiatives. By addressing bottlenecks in the sales funnel, we aim to increase overall conversion rates, resulting in sustainable revenue growth."

Engaging Your Audience:

11. Building Tension:

- "As we reveal challenges and conflicts in the data, we build tension. Stakeholders eagerly anticipate resolutions and strategic recommendations."

12. Climax and Resolution:

- "The climax is our proposed action plan. By optimizing the customer journey, refocusing marketing efforts, and capitalizing on successful product lines, we pave the way for a resolution to our sales plateau."

Iterative Refinement:

13. Feedback Loop:

- "Before finalizing this narrative, we seek feedback. Does this story resonate? Are there additional elements stakeholders wish to explore? This feedback loop ensures the narrative is tailored to meet the specific needs of our audience."

14. Continuous Improvement:

- "As we embark on this journey of data storytelling, it's crucial to view it as an iterative process. New data, changing business goals, and evolving market conditions will prompt us to continuously refine and enhance our narrative."

In this example, the narrative weaves together data insights, humanizes the challenges faced, and engages stakeholders through interactive elements. The story is tailored to the unique perspectives of the sales team and executive leadership, ultimately delivering a compelling and actionable analysis of sales performance.

5.3.2 Engaging Stakeholders through Storytelling

In the realm of data analysis, storytelling transcends the mere presentation of facts and figures. It is a strategic approach to convey complex information in a compelling and relatable manner. In this section, we delve into the nuances of engaging stakeholders through storytelling, exploring techniques to capture their attention, foster understanding, and drive meaningful action.

 # 1. Recognizing the Importance of Stakeholder Engagement

1.1 From Analysis to Action:

- Acknowledge that the ultimate goal of data analysis is not just to inform but to inspire action. Stakeholder engagement is the catalyst that transforms data insights into tangible outcomes.

1.2 Building Connections:

- Understand that stakeholders may come from diverse backgrounds and possess varying levels of familiarity with data. Effective storytelling bridges these gaps, fostering a connection between the analyst and the audience.

1.3 Aligning with Organizational Goals:

- Tailor your storytelling to align with the broader goals and mission of the organization. Demonstrating how data insights contribute to overarching objectives enhances stakeholder buy-in.

 # 2. Elements of Engaging Data Storytelling

2.1 Compelling Characters:

- Introduce 'characters' within the data story. These can be specific products, customer segments, or even individual team members. Humanizing the data makes it relatable and memorable.

2.2 Emotional Resonance:

- Infuse emotion into the narrative. Connect data points to real-world scenarios that evoke empathy, enthusiasm, or concern. Emotions amplify the impact of the story and make it more memorable.

2.3 Clear Conflict and Resolution:

- Define a clear conflict within the data—be it challenges, bottlenecks, or missed opportunities. The resolution, supported by data insights, forms the crux of the story, providing a satisfying arc for stakeholders.

2.4 Visual Appeal:

- Leverage visually appealing elements, such as captivating charts, impactful images, and color schemes that evoke specific emotions. Visual appeal enhances engagement and aids in conveying complex information.

 # 3. Techniques for Engaging Stakeholders

3.1 Interactive Elements:

- Incorporate interactive elements within your presentation or dashboard. Allow stakeholders to explore specific data points, drill down into details, and derive insights tailored to their interests.

3.2 Anecdotes and Case Studies:

- Share anecdotes or case studies that illustrate the impact of data-driven decisions. Real-life examples resonate with stakeholders, making the data more tangible and actionable.

3.3 Personalization:

- Personalize the story to the audience. Tailor the narrative to address the concerns, priorities, and interests of specific stakeholders. A personalized approach enhances relevance and engagement.

 # 4. Crafting a Compelling Data Narrative

4.1 Beginning with Impact:

- Start the narrative with a compelling impact statement. Capture stakeholders' attention by immediately highlighting the significance of the insights and their potential ramifications.

4.2 Logical Flow:

- Ensure a logical flow in your narrative. Each segment should seamlessly transition to the next, guiding stakeholders through the story without causing confusion or cognitive overload.

4.3 Highlighting Successes:

- Celebrate successes and positive outcomes. Demonstrating how previous data-driven decisions led to favorable results instills confidence and enthusiasm among stakeholders.

 # 5. Tailoring to Stakeholder Roles

5.1 Executive Leadership:

- For executives, focus on high-level insights that align with strategic goals. Emphasize the potential impact on key performance indicators and overall business objectives.

5.2 Operational Teams:

- Operational teams may benefit from more granular insights. Tailor the storytelling to address specific challenges they face and provide actionable recommendations for improvement.

6. Continuous Engagement

6.1 Post-Presentation Follow-Up:

- Engage stakeholders beyond the initial presentation. Follow up with additional insights, clarifications, or opportunities for further exploration. This reinforces ongoing engagement.

6.2 Feedback Mechanisms:

- Establish feedback mechanisms to gauge stakeholder reactions and insights. Understanding their perspectives allows for continuous improvement in the storytelling approach.

7. Case Study: Transformative Marketing Insights

7.1 Context Setting:

- "Our marketing analysis unveils transformative insights into customer behavior and preferences. The story begins with the challenge of declining customer engagement."

7.2 Compelling Characters:

- "Meet our characters—distinct customer segments with unique preferences. Their journey through our products shapes the narrative, making it relatable."

7.3 Interactive Elements:

- "Within our interactive dashboard, stakeholders can explore how adjusting marketing strategies for specific customer segments resulted in increased engagement and sales."

7.4 Emotional Resonance:

- "As we dive into customer feedback and testimonials, emotions surface. Stakeholders connect emotionally, understanding the impact of tailored marketing efforts on individual customers."

 # Conclusion: A Call to Action through Storytelling

In conclusion, engaging stakeholders through storytelling is an art that transforms data analysis into a compelling narrative. By understanding the elements of effective storytelling, leveraging interactive elements, and tailoring the narrative to the audience, analysts can foster a deeper connection with stakeholders. Continuous engagement and a focus on actionable insights ensure that the story leads to meaningful outcomes, driving positive change within the organization.

Illustrative Example: Transformative Marketing Insights Story

Context Setting:

Imagine you are a data analyst presenting transformative marketing insights to stakeholders. The goal is to engage them through storytelling, providing a clear narrative around the challenges faced, the characters involved, and the impact of data-driven decisions.

1. Beginning with Impact:

- "Our marketing analysis reveals a pivotal moment — a decline in customer engagement. This isn't just a data point; it's a call to action. The impact is clear: diminishing brand connection and potential revenue loss."

2. Compelling Characters:

- "Meet our characters—the 'Loyalists,' 'Explorers,' and 'Price-Conscious.' These distinct customer segments shape our narrative. Each character has unique preferences, behaviors, and reactions to our marketing strategies."

3. Interactive Elements:

- "Within our interactive dashboard, stakeholders can dynamically explore how each marketing campaign resonates with different segments. Clicking on a segment reveals detailed insights—how 'Loyalists' responded to personalized content, for instance."

4. Emotional Resonance:

- "As we delve into customer feedback and testimonials, emotions surface. Picture Mary, a 'Loyalist,' expressing gratitude for the personalized recommendations. Emotions become integral to the story, conveying the impact of tailored marketing efforts on individual customers."

5. Conflict and Resolution:

- "Our conflict? A decline in overall engagement. The resolution emerges as we identify the marketing strategies that resonate most with each segment. By resolving this conflict, we pave the way for increased engagement and brand loyalty."

6. Highlighting Successes:

- "Celebrating successes is crucial. With our newfound insights, we implemented personalized campaigns, resulting in a 15% increase in engagement across all segments. The story celebrates these victories, reinforcing the power of data-driven decisions."

7. Logical Flow:

- "Our narrative follows a logical flow. We started with the challenge, introduced our characters, explored their responses to marketing efforts, and culminated in a resolution—increased engagement and a pathway for sustained growth."

8. Tailoring to Stakeholder Roles:

- "For our executive leaders, the narrative emphasizes the strategic impact on brand perception and revenue growth. Operational teams gain granular insights into campaign effectiveness for day-to-day decision-making."

9. Continuous Engagement:

- "Our story doesn't end with this presentation. We initiate continuous engagement by offering stakeholders opportunities to explore the dashboard independently, encouraging them to uncover additional insights and share their perspectives."

10. Feedback Mechanisms:

- "To ensure the ongoing relevance of our story, we establish feedback mechanisms. We want to hear stakeholders' reactions, insights, and suggestions for improvement. This iterative approach ensures our narrative remains impactful."

This illustrative example showcases how storytelling transforms data analysis into a captivating journey. By introducing characters, leveraging interactive elements, and conveying emotional resonance, stakeholders become not just passive observers of data but active participants in the narrative, driving positive change within the marketing strategy.

CHAPTER VI
Advanced Analytics in Python and R

6.1 Introduction to Python and R for Data Analysis

6.1.1 Installing and Setting Up Python and R

Introduction:

In the realm of advanced analytics, proficiency in programming languages such as Python and R is paramount. This section guides you through the process of installing and setting up Python and R, laying the foundation for harnessing their robust capabilities in data analysis.

1. Python Installation and Configuration

1.1 Installing Python:

- Begin by visiting the official Python website (https://www.python.org/) to download the latest version of Python. The website provides installers for various operating systems, ensuring compatibility with Windows, macOS, and Linux.

- During installation, be sure to check the box that says "Add Python to PATH." This ensures that Python can be easily accessed from the command line.

1.2 Choosing an Integrated Development Environment (IDE):

- Consider using popular Python IDEs such as Jupyter Notebooks, VSCode, or PyCharm. These environments provide a user-friendly interface, code autocompletion, and visualization capabilities, enhancing the overall development experience.

1.3 Package Management with Pip:

- Python's package manager, pip, facilitates the installation of additional libraries and packages. After installing Python, open the command prompt or terminal and run `pip install package_name` to install desired packages.

1.4 Virtual Environments:

- Embrace virtual environments to isolate project dependencies. Use `venv` or `virtualenv` to create a virtual environment, ensuring project-specific package versions and preventing conflicts between different projects.

2. R Installation and Configuration

2.1 Installing R:

- Visit the Comprehensive R Archive Network (CRAN) website (https://cran.r-project.org/) to download and install R. The installation process is straightforward and available for Windows, macOS, and Linux.

2.2 Choosing an IDE:

- RStudio is a popular IDE for R, offering a user-friendly interface, integrated tools for plotting, debugging, and package management. Download and install RStudio to enhance your R coding experience.

2.3 Package Installation with install.packages:

- R uses the `install.packages` function to install additional packages. For example, to install the 'dplyr' package, run `install.packages("dplyr")` in the R console.

2.4 Managing Packages with library:

- Once installed, load packages into your R environment using the `library` function. For the 'dplyr' package, use `library(dplyr)` to make its functions available for use.

3. Basic Data Manipulation in Python and R

3.1 Python with Pandas:

- Introduce Pandas, a powerful Python library for data manipulation. Showcase fundamental data structures: Series and DataFrame. Demonstrate basic operations such as data selection, filtering, and aggregation using Pandas.

```python
import pandas as pd

# Creating a DataFrame
data = {'Name': ['Alice', 'Bob', 'Charlie'],
        'Age': [25, 30, 35],
        'City': ['New York', 'San Francisco', 'Los Angeles']}

df = pd.DataFrame(data)

# Displaying the DataFrame
```

```
print(df)
```

3.2 R with dplyr:

- Introduce the 'dplyr' package in R for data manipulation. Cover key functions such as `select`, `filter`, `arrange`, and `mutate` for efficiently manipulating data frames in R.

```R
library(dplyr)

# Creating a tibble (modern data frame in R)
data <- tibble(
  Name = c("Alice", "Bob", "Charlie"),
  Age = c(25, 30, 35),
  City = c("New York", "San Francisco", "Los Angeles")
)

# Displaying the tibble
print(data)
```

4. Best Practices for Installation and Setup

4.1 Regular Updates:

- Regularly update Python and R installations to access the latest features, security patches, and bug fixes. Utilize package managers (`pip` and `install.packages`) to keep libraries up to date.

4.2 Documentation and Community Support:

- Refer to official documentation for Python (https://docs.python.org/) and R (https://www.r-project.org/other-docs.html) for detailed information on installation and usage. Engage with vibrant online communities to seek assistance and stay informed about best practices.

4.3 Version Control:

- Implement version control using tools like Git for both Python and R projects. This ensures traceability and facilitates collaboration, especially when working on larger projects or within a team.

5. Troubleshooting and Common Issues

5.1 Path Configuration:

- If encountering issues with PATH configurations, revisit installation steps to ensure Python and R are added to the system PATH. This resolves common problems related to accessing Python and R from the command line.

5.2 Dependency Conflicts:

- In Python, use virtual environments to manage dependencies and avoid conflicts between project requirements. For R, pay attention to package versions to prevent compatibility issues.

6. Conclusion: Empowering Data Analysis with Python and R

In conclusion, the seamless installation and setup of Python and R lay the groundwork for advanced analytics and data manipulation. Whether leveraging Pandas in Python or dplyr in R, these languages empower data analysts with versatile tools to explore, analyze, and derive insights from complex datasets. By following best practices, staying engaged with communities, and troubleshooting effectively, analysts can unlock the full potential of Python and R in their data analysis journey.

6.1.2 Basic Data Manipulation in Python and R

Data manipulation forms the foundation of any data analysis endeavor, and proficiency in basic manipulation techniques is essential for extracting meaningful insights from datasets. In this section, we explore the fundamental skills required for data manipulation in both Python and R, focusing on common tasks such as data loading, subsetting, filtering, and transforming.

1. Loading Data

1.1 Python (Using Pandas):

- Pandas, a powerful data manipulation library in Python, provides functions to read various data formats. The `read_csv` function is commonly used for reading CSV files.

```python
import pandas as pd

# Reading a CSV file into a DataFrame
df = pd.read_csv('your_dataset.csv')
```

1.2 R:

- In R, the `read.csv` function is used to read CSV files into a data frame.

```R
# Reading a CSV file into a data frame
df <- read.csv('your_dataset.csv')
```

2. Subsetting Data

2.1 Python (Using Pandas):

- Pandas allows for easy subsetting of data using column names or conditions.

```python
# Selecting specific columns
selected_columns = df[['Column1', 'Column2']]

# Filtering rows based on a condition
filtered_rows = df[df['Column1'] > 50]
```

2.2 R:

- In R, data frame subsetting is achieved similarly.

```R
# Selecting specific columns
selected_columns <- df[, c('Column1', 'Column2')]

# Filtering rows based on a condition
filtered_rows <- df[df$Column1 > 50, ]
```

3. Handling Missing Data

3.1 Python (Using Pandas):

- Pandas provides methods to handle missing data, including the `dropna` and `fillna` functions.

```python
# Dropping rows with missing values
df_cleaned = df.dropna()

# Imputing missing values with the mean
df_imputed = df.fillna(df.mean())
```

3.2 R:

- In R, missing values can be handled using functions like `complete.cases` and `na.omit`.

```R
# Dropping rows with missing values
df_cleaned <- df[complete.cases(df), ]

# Imputing missing values with the mean
df_imputed <- df
df_imputed$Column1[is.na(df_imputed$Column1)] <- mean(df_imputed$Column1,
na.rm = TRUE)
```

4. Transforming Data

4.1 Python (Using Pandas):

- Pandas provides versatile tools for data transformation, including creating new columns and applying functions.

```python
# Creating a new column based on existing columns
df['NewColumn'] = df['Column1'] + df['Column2']

# Applying a function to a column
df['TransformedColumn'] = df['OriginalColumn'].apply(lambda x: x  2)
```

4.2 R:

- In R, data transformation involves creating new variables and applying functions.

```R
# Creating a new column based on existing columns
df$NewColumn <- df$Column1 + df$Column2

# Applying a function to a column
df$TransformedColumn <- lapply(df$OriginalColumn, function(x) x  2)
```

5. Aggregating Data

5.1 Python (Using Pandas):

- Pandas simplifies the aggregation process using functions like `groupby` and `agg`.

```python
# Grouping by a column and calculating mean
grouped_data = df.groupby('GroupingColumn').agg({'NumericColumn': 'mean'})
```

5.2 R:

- In R, the `aggregate` function is commonly used for data aggregation.

```R
# Grouping by a column and calculating mean
aggregated_data <- aggregate(NumericColumn ~ GroupingColumn, data=df, FUN=mean)
```

6. Merging and Joining DataFrames

6.1 Python (Using Pandas):

- Merging dataframes in Pandas is straightforward with the `merge` function.

```python
# Merging two dataframes on a common column
merged_df = pd.merge(df1, df2, on='CommonColumn', how='inner')
```

6.2 R:

- In R, the `merge` function is used for joining dataframes.

```R
# Merging two dataframes on a common column
merged_df <- merge(df1, df2, by='CommonColumn', all=FALSE)
```

7. Conclusion: Building a Strong Foundation

Mastering basic data manipulation techniques in Python and R lays the groundwork for effective data analysis. These skills are vital for handling diverse datasets, ensuring data quality, and preparing data for advanced analytical tasks. As we progress into more advanced analytics, a solid foundation in data manipulation becomes increasingly crucial for deriving meaningful insights from complex datasets.

6.2 Advanced Analytical Libraries

6.2.1 Pandas for Data Manipulation

In the expansive landscape of data analysis, the ability to manipulate and transform data efficiently is a cornerstone skill. Pandas, a powerful Python library, emerges as a versatile tool for data manipulation. This section delves into the intricacies of Pandas, exploring its key features and functions that empower analysts to wrangle and shape data with precision.

1. Introduction to Pandas

1.1 Overview:

- Pandas is an open-source data manipulation and analysis library for Python. It provides high-performance, easy-to-use data structures such as DataFrame and Series, along with a vast array of functions for data cleaning, exploration, and transformation.

1.2 Installation:

- Install Pandas using the standard Python package manager, pip. Execute `pip install pandas` in the command line to ensure the library is readily available for use in your Python environment.

2. Pandas Data Structures

2.1 DataFrame:

- The DataFrame is Pandas' fundamental data structure, representing a two-dimensional, tabular data structure with labeled axes (rows and columns). It is akin to a spreadsheet or SQL table.

```python
import pandas as pd

# Creating a DataFrame from a dictionary
data = {'Name': ['Alice', 'Bob', 'Charlie'],
    'Age': [25, 30, 35],
    'City': ['New York', 'San Francisco', 'Los Angeles']}

df = pd.DataFrame(data)
```

2.2 Series:

- A Series is a one-dimensional labeled array capable of holding any data type. It can be seen as a single column of a DataFrame.

```python
# Creating a Series
ages = pd.Series([25, 30, 35], name='Age')
```

3. Essential Data Manipulation Operations

3.1 Selecting and Filtering Data:

- Pandas provides multiple methods for selecting and filtering data, including boolean indexing and conditional selection.

```python
# Selecting a column
name_column = df['Name']

# Filtering rows based on a condition
filtered_rows = df[df['Age'] > 30]
```

3.2 Sorting and Arranging Data:

- Sorting data can be achieved using the `sort_values` method. It allows sorting based on one or more columns.

```python
# Sorting by 'Age' in ascending order
sorted_df = df.sort_values(by='Age')
```

3.3 Adding and Mutating Columns:

- Pandas simplifies adding and mutating columns, enhancing the DataFrame with new information.

```python
# Creating a new column 'Age_Group'
df['Age_Group'] = pd.cut(df['Age'], bins=[0, 30, 40, float('inf')], labels=['<30', '30-40', '40+'])
```

4. Grouping and Aggregating Data

4.1 Grouping Data:

- Pandas enables grouping data based on one or more columns. This is pivotal for performing aggregate operations on subsets of data.

```python
# Grouping by 'City' and calculating average age
grouped_data = df.groupby('City')['Age'].mean()
```

4.2 Aggregating Data:

- Aggregation functions such as `sum`, `mean`, and `count` allow summarizing data within groups.

```python
```

```
# Aggregating data by summing values within each group
aggregated_data = df.groupby('City').agg({'Age': 'sum', 'Name': 'count'})
```

5. Handling Missing Data

5.1 Identifying Missing Data:

- Pandas facilitates the identification of missing data using methods like `isnull()` and `notnull()`.

```python
# Checking for missing values
missing_values = df.isnull()
```

5.2 Handling Missing Data:

- Strategies for handling missing data include removal, imputation, or interpolation.

```python
# Dropping rows with missing values
df_cleaned = df.dropna()

# Imputing missing values with the mean
```

```
df_imputed = df.fillna(df.mean())
```

6. Merging and Concatenating DataFrames

6.1 Merging DataFrames:

- Merging combines DataFrames based on common columns, offering flexibility in combining information.

```python
# Merging two DataFrames on 'ID'
merged_df = pd.merge(df1, df2, on='ID', how='inner')
```

6.2 Concatenating DataFrames:

- Concatenation appends DataFrames along a particular axis, either rows or columns.

```python
# Concatenating two DataFrames vertically
concatenated_df = pd.concat([df1, df2], axis=0)
```

7. Conclusion: Pandas Mastery for Data Manipulation

Mastering Pandas for data manipulation empowers data analysts to efficiently preprocess, clean, and transform data. The library's rich functionality, combined with its intuitive syntax, makes it an indispensable tool in the data analyst's toolkit. As we advance into the realm of advanced analytics, a solid foundation in Pandas sets the stage for more intricate analyses and insights.

6.2.2 Scikit-learn for Machine Learning

Machine learning, a transformative field within data analysis, empowers analysts to build predictive models and uncover patterns in data. Scikit-learn, a powerful machine learning library in Python, stands as a cornerstone for implementing a wide range of machine learning algorithms. In this section, we delve into the functionalities of Scikit-learn, exploring its capabilities, common algorithms, and best practices for building effective machine learning models.

1. Introduction to Scikit-learn

1.1 Overview:

- Scikit-learn is an open-source machine learning library for Python, designed to provide simple and efficient tools for data analysis and modeling. It builds on other popular scientific computing libraries such as NumPy, SciPy, and Matplotlib, creating a cohesive ecosystem for machine learning tasks.

1.2 Installation:

- Install Scikit-learn using pip, the Python package manager. Execute `pip install scikit-learn` in the command line to ensure the library is readily available for your machine learning projects.

2. Key Functionalities of Scikit-learn

2.1 Data Preprocessing:

- Scikit-learn provides robust tools for preprocessing data, including handling missing values, scaling features, and encoding categorical variables.

```python
from sklearn.impute import SimpleImputer
from sklearn.preprocessing import StandardScaler, OneHotEncoder
from sklearn.compose import ColumnTransformer
from sklearn.pipeline import Pipeline

# Example pipeline for preprocessing
numeric_features = ['Age', 'Income']
categorical_features = ['Gender', 'Education']

numeric_transformer = Pipeline(steps=[
    ('imputer', SimpleImputer(strategy='mean')),
    ('scaler', StandardScaler())
])

categorical_transformer = Pipeline(steps=[
    ('imputer', SimpleImputer(strategy='most_frequent')),
```

```
    ('onehot', OneHotEncoder(handle_unknown='ignore'))
])

preprocessor = ColumnTransformer(
    transformers=[
        ('num', numeric_transformer, numeric_features),
        ('cat', categorical_transformer, categorical_features)
    ])
```

2.2 Supervised Learning:

- Scikit-learn supports a wide range of supervised learning algorithms, including linear regression, support vector machines, decision trees, and ensemble methods like random forests.

```python
from sklearn.model_selection import train_test_split
from sklearn.ensemble import RandomForestClassifier
from sklearn.metrics import accuracy_score

# Splitting data into training and testing sets
X_train, X_test, y_train, y_test = train_test_split(X, y, test_size=0.2, random_state=42)

# Creating and training a Random Forest classifier
```

```
clf = RandomForestClassifier(n_estimators=100, random_state=42)
clf.fit(X_train, y_train)

# Making predictions on the test set
predictions = clf.predict(X_test)

# Evaluating model accuracy
accuracy = accuracy_score(y_test, predictions)
```

2.3 Unsupervised Learning:

- Unsupervised learning algorithms, such as clustering and dimensionality reduction, are also well-supported in Scikit-learn.

```python
from sklearn.cluster import KMeans
from sklearn.decomposition import PCA

# Clustering with KMeans
kmeans = KMeans(n_clusters=3, random_state=42)
clusters = kmeans.fit_predict(X)

# Dimensionality reduction with PCA
```

```
pca = PCA(n_components=2)

reduced_data = pca.fit_transform(X)
```

2.4 Model Evaluation and Hyperparameter Tuning:

- Scikit-learn facilitates model evaluation through metrics such as accuracy, precision, recall, and F1 score. Additionally, tools for hyperparameter tuning, such as GridSearchCV, streamline the process of finding optimal model configurations.

```python
from sklearn.model_selection import GridSearchCV


# Define hyperparameter grid

param_grid = {'n_estimators': [50, 100, 150],

          'max_depth': [None, 10, 20]}


# Create a Random Forest classifier

clf = RandomForestClassifier(random_state=42)


# Perform grid search for hyperparameter tuning

grid_search = GridSearchCV(clf, param_grid, cv=5, scoring='accuracy')

grid_search.fit(X_train, y_train)


# Best hyperparameters and corresponding accuracy
```

```
best_params = grid_search.best_params_

best_accuracy = grid_search.best_score_
```

3. Building a Machine Learning Pipeline with Scikit-learn

3.1 Pipeline Construction:

- Scikit-learn encourages the use of pipelines to streamline the machine learning workflow. Pipelines sequentially apply a list of transformations and a final estimator.

```python
from sklearn.pipeline import Pipeline


# Example pipeline combining preprocessing and classification

pipeline = Pipeline([

    ('preprocessor', preprocessor),

    ('classifier', RandomForestClassifier())

])


# Fit the model using the pipeline

pipeline.fit(X_train, y_train)


# Make predictions using the pipeline
```

```
predictions = pipeline.predict(X_test)
```

3.2 Cross-Validation with Pipelines:

- Pipelines seamlessly integrate with cross-validation techniques, ensuring robust model evaluation.

```python
from sklearn.model_selection import cross_val_score

# Perform cross-validation using the pipeline
cv_scores = cross_val_score(pipeline, X, y, cv=5, scoring='accuracy')
```

4. Handling Imbalanced Data and Advanced Techniques

4.1 Dealing with Imbalanced Data:

- Scikit-learn provides tools to address imbalanced class distributions, including resampling techniques and specialized algorithms.

```python
from imblearn.over_sampling import SMOTE
from sklearn.ensemble import BalancedRandomForestClassifier
```

```
# Applying SMOTE for oversampling
smote = SMOTE(random_state=42)
X_resampled, y_resampled = smote.fit_resample(X, y)

# Using BalancedRandomForestClassifier for imbalanced data
balanced_clf = BalancedRandomForestClassifier(n_estimators=100, random_state=42)
balanced_clf.fit(X_resampled, y_resampled)
```

4.2 Advanced Techniques:

- Scikit-learn supports advanced techniques such as ensemble methods, stacking, and feature engineering for enhanced model performance.

```python
from sklearn.ensemble import StackingClassifier
from sklearn.ensemble import GradientBoostingClassifier
from sklearn.linear_model import LogisticRegression

# Stacking classifier with a base Random Forest and Gradient Boosting
base_classifiers = [('rf', RandomForestClassifier(n_estimators=100, random_state=42)),
                    ('gb', GradientBoostingClassifier(n_estimators=100, random_state=42))]

stacking_clf = StackingClassifier(estimators=base_classifiers,
final_estimator=LogisticRegression())
```

```
stacking_clf.fit(X_train, y_train)
```

5. Best Practices and Conclusion

5.1 Best Practices in Scikit-learn:

- Follow best practices such as feature scaling, proper data splitting, and robust model evaluation to ensure reliable and reproducible results.

5.2 Conclusion: Mastering Machine Learning with Scikit-learn:

- Scikit-learn serves as a versatile and user-friendly library for machine learning in Python. Mastering its functionalities equips data analysts with the tools needed to explore and implement a myriad of machine learning techniques. As the journey into advanced analytics continues, Scikit-learn stands as an invaluable companion, enabling the creation of robust, predictive models and uncovering insights within complex datasets.

CHAPTER VII
Real-world Applications and Case Studies

7.1 Applying Data Analysis in Business

7.1.1 Marketing Analytics

In the ever-evolving landscape of business, Marketing Analytics stands out as a crucial tool for organizations seeking a competitive edge. This section delves into the intricacies of applying data analysis techniques specifically within the realm of marketing.

Understanding the Power of Marketing Analytics

Marketing Analytics harnesses the power of data to uncover valuable insights into consumer behavior, preferences, and trends. By leveraging statistical analysis, machine learning algorithms, and data visualization tools, businesses can gain a deeper understanding of their target audience and optimize their marketing strategies.

Segmentation and Targeting

One of the key aspects of Marketing Analytics is segmentation – the process of dividing the target market into distinct groups based on demographics, behavior, or other relevant criteria. Through data-driven segmentation, businesses can tailor their marketing efforts to specific audience segments, delivering personalized and more effective campaigns.

Campaign Effectiveness Measurement

Marketing campaigns generate vast amounts of data, ranging from click-through rates and conversion rates to social media engagement metrics. Analyzing this data provides invaluable insights into the effectiveness of different campaigns. Marketers can identify which strategies resonate with their audience, allowing for data-driven adjustments and optimizations.

Customer Lifetime Value (CLV) Analysis

Understanding the long-term value of a customer is pivotal for sustainable business growth. Marketing Analytics enables businesses to calculate and analyze Customer Lifetime Value, helping them allocate resources effectively, identify high-value customers, and devise strategies to enhance customer retention.

Predictive Modeling for Market Trends

Anticipating market trends is a game-changer in the dynamic world of marketing. Through predictive modeling, businesses can forecast future trends based on historical data. This proactive approach empowers marketers to stay ahead of the curve, adapt strategies in real-time, and capitalize on emerging opportunities.

Challenges and Considerations

While Marketing Analytics offers immense potential, it is not without challenges. Privacy concerns, data quality issues, and the need for skilled analysts are hurdles that businesses must navigate. This section explores these challenges and provides insights into mitigating risks while maximizing the benefits of Marketing Analytics.

Case Studies: Real-world Applications of Marketing Analytics

To illustrate the practical application of Marketing Analytics, this section includes case studies that showcase successful implementations across diverse industries. From e-commerce platforms optimizing their ad spend to brick-and-mortar retailers enhancing customer engagement, these case studies provide a comprehensive understanding of how businesses can leverage Marketing Analytics to achieve tangible results.

As we explore Marketing Analytics in detail, the overarching goal is to empower businesses to make informed decisions, foster innovation, and achieve sustainable growth in today's data-driven business landscape.

7.1.2 Financial Analysis

Financial Analysis, a pivotal component of data-driven decision-making in the business realm, plays a critical role in assessing the fiscal health and performance of organizations. In this section, we delve into the nuanced world of Financial Analysis and explore how data analysis techniques can be harnessed for strategic financial insights.

The Essence of Financial Analysis

Financial Analysis involves scrutinizing financial statements, market trends, and economic indicators to evaluate an organization's financial performance and make informed decisions. Data analysis techniques provide a systematic approach to interpret financial data, enabling stakeholders to identify strengths, weaknesses, opportunities, and threats.

Key Metrics and Ratios

Understanding and interpreting financial metrics and ratios are fundamental to Financial Analysis. This section delves into key indicators such as liquidity ratios, profitability ratios, and leverage ratios. Through data-driven calculations and comparisons, organizations gain a comprehensive view of their financial standing, aiding in strategic planning and risk management.

Trend Analysis and Forecasting

Financial data extends beyond static numbers; it tells a story of an organization's journey. Trend analysis involves scrutinizing historical financial data to identify patterns and trends. Moreover, predictive modeling techniques empower businesses to forecast future financial scenarios, facilitating proactive decision-making and risk mitigation.

Risk Management through Data Analysis

Financial Analysis is integral to identifying and managing risks. By leveraging statistical models and scenario analysis, organizations can assess the potential impact of various risks on their financial health. This proactive approach enables the development of risk mitigation strategies to safeguard the organization's financial stability.

Performance Benchmarking and Competitive Analysis

Comparative analysis is a cornerstone of Financial Analysis. Data-driven benchmarking allows organizations to compare their financial performance against industry peers and competitors. This section explores how businesses can gain a competitive edge by identifying areas for improvement, setting performance benchmarks, and aligning financial strategies with industry best practices.

Integration of External Data Sources

In the era of big data, Financial Analysis extends beyond internal datasets. Integrating external data sources, such as market trends, economic indicators, and geopolitical factors, enriches the analysis. This holistic approach provides a more comprehensive understanding of the external forces shaping financial landscapes.

Challenges and Ethical Considerations

While the benefits of Financial Analysis are substantial, challenges such as data accuracy, data privacy, and ethical considerations must be addressed. This section delves into the ethical implications of financial data analysis and explores strategies for ensuring responsible and transparent practices.

Case Studies: Practical Applications of Financial Analysis

To illustrate the real-world applications of Financial Analysis, this section includes case studies that showcase successful implementations across diverse industries. From risk management strategies to financial forecasting precision, these case studies offer insights into how organizations leverage Financial Analysis to drive success.

As we navigate the intricacies of Financial Analysis, the goal is to equip businesses with the tools and insights needed to navigate the complexities of the financial landscape and make strategic decisions that contribute to long-term success.

7.1.3 Operations and Supply Chain Analytics

Operations and Supply Chain Analytics represent the convergence of data analysis and logistics, providing businesses with the tools to optimize processes, enhance efficiency, and ensure the seamless flow of goods and services. In this section, we explore the multifaceted realm of Operations and Supply Chain Analytics, unraveling how data-driven insights revolutionize the management of intricate business networks.

Strategic Importance of Operations and Supply Chain Analytics

Operations and Supply Chain Analytics play a pivotal role in the strategic decision-making process for organizations operating in a globalized and interconnected business environment. By harnessing data analysis techniques, businesses can gain visibility into their supply chain, identify bottlenecks, and streamline operations for maximum efficiency.

Demand Forecasting and Inventory Management

One of the fundamental challenges in operations is predicting and managing demand. Through advanced data analysis, businesses can develop robust demand forecasting models, taking into account historical data, market trends, and external factors. Accurate forecasting facilitates optimized inventory management, ensuring that products are available when and where they are needed, minimizing excess inventory costs.

Supply Chain Optimization and Efficiency

Supply chains can be complex, involving multiple stakeholders, transportation modes, and distribution channels. Operations and Supply Chain Analytics enable businesses to optimize these networks, identifying the most efficient routes, minimizing lead times, and reducing overall operational costs. Real-time data analysis allows for agile decision-making, especially in dynamic environments.

Quality Control and Process Improvement

Data analysis facilitates continuous improvement in operational processes. By monitoring key performance indicators (KPIs) and employing statistical methods, businesses can identify areas for improvement in quality control and overall process efficiency. This iterative approach contributes to a culture of continuous improvement within the organization.

Risk Management and Resilience

The modern business landscape is rife with uncertainties, from natural disasters to geopolitical events. Operations and Supply Chain Analytics empower organizations to assess and mitigate risks effectively. Through scenario analysis and predictive modeling, businesses can develop contingency plans, ensuring resilience in the face of unforeseen challenges.

Technology Integration in Operations

The advent of Industry 4.0 has ushered in a new era of technology integration in operations. From the Internet of Things (IoT) to artificial intelligence, businesses are leveraging cutting-edge technologies to enhance visibility, automate processes, and make data-driven decisions. This section explores the transformative impact of technology on operations and supply chain management.

Challenges and Considerations

While Operations and Supply Chain Analytics offer significant advantages, they are not without challenges. This section addresses issues such as data silos, interoperability, and the need for skilled personnel. Navigating these challenges is crucial for organizations looking to fully capitalize on the potential of data-driven operations.

Case Studies: Real-world Applications of Operations and Supply Chain Analytics

To illustrate the practical application of Operations and Supply Chain Analytics, this section includes case studies highlighting successful implementations across diverse industries. From improving logistics efficiency to mitigating supply chain disruptions, these cases showcase how businesses leverage data analysis to drive operational excellence.

As we explore the intricacies of Operations and Supply Chain Analytics, the objective is to empower businesses to optimize their processes, enhance resilience, and navigate the complexities of today's interconnected global supply chains with confidence and precision.

7.2 Case Studies

7.2.1 Solving Business Problems with Data

In the dynamic landscape of modern business, the ability to harness the power of data for problem-solving is a defining factor for organizational success. This section delves into various case studies that exemplify how businesses across different industries leverage data analysis to address complex challenges and drive strategic decision-making.

1. Improving Customer Retention in E-commerce

Problem Statement: A leading e-commerce platform was facing challenges with customer retention. High bounce rates and a decline in repeat purchases prompted the need for data-driven solutions.

Data Analysis Approach: The team conducted a thorough analysis of customer behavior data, identifying patterns and factors contributing to churn. Machine learning algorithms were employed to predict customer churn probabilities.

Outcome: The e-commerce platform implemented targeted marketing campaigns based on the identified patterns, personalized recommendations, and loyalty programs. The result was a significant improvement in customer retention rates and a subsequent increase in overall revenue.

2. Supply Chain Optimization in Manufacturing

Problem Statement: A manufacturing company was grappling with inefficiencies in its supply chain, leading to delays, excess inventory, and increased operational costs.

Data Analysis Approach: Utilizing Operations and Supply Chain Analytics, the company analyzed historical data, identified bottlenecks, and optimized its supply chain routes. Predictive modeling was employed to anticipate demand fluctuations.

Outcome: The company achieved a streamlined supply chain, reducing lead times and minimizing excess inventory. The data-driven approach enhanced overall operational efficiency and responsiveness to market demand.

3. Fraud Detection in Financial Transactions

Problem Statement: A financial institution faced challenges with fraudulent transactions impacting the security of its customers and the integrity of its services.

Data Analysis Approach: The institution implemented advanced analytics techniques to analyze transactional data in real-time. Machine learning models were trained to detect patterns indicative of fraudulent activities.

Outcome: The proactive fraud detection system successfully identified and prevented fraudulent transactions, safeguarding both the institution and its customers. This not only protected financial assets but also enhanced customer trust.

4. Healthcare Resource Allocation in a Pandemic

Problem Statement: A healthcare system was overwhelmed during a pandemic, struggling with resource allocation, including bed availability, medical supplies, and staffing.

Data Analysis Approach: The healthcare system utilized data analytics to model the spread of the virus, predict patient admissions, and optimize resource allocation based on real-time data.

Outcome: By leveraging data-driven insights, the healthcare system effectively allocated resources, ensuring that critical care was provided where it was needed most. This approach played a crucial role in managing the impact of the pandemic on healthcare services.

5. Improving Employee Productivity in a Tech Company

Problem Statement: A technology company observed a decline in employee productivity and sought to identify underlying factors impacting workforce efficiency.

Data Analysis Approach: Employee performance data, collaboration patterns, and work hours were analyzed. Machine learning algorithms were employed to identify correlations between certain factors and productivity levels.

Outcome: The company implemented targeted training programs, adjusted work schedules based on peak productivity hours, and fostered a collaborative work environment. Employee productivity saw a notable improvement, positively impacting overall company performance.

These case studies underscore the versatility and transformative potential of data analysis in solving diverse business problems. Whether it's enhancing customer experience, optimizing operations, ensuring security, managing crises, or boosting workforce efficiency, data-driven solutions prove instrumental in navigating the complexities of the modern business landscape. As organizations continue to evolve, the role of data analysis in problem-solving remains an indispensable tool for driving innovation and sustainable growth.

Certainly! Let's dive into a more detailed example with specific numerical data to illustrate the impact of data analysis on optimizing digital marketing campaigns in e-commerce.

Case Study: Optimizing Digital Marketing Campaigns in E-commerce

Problem Statement:

XYZ Mart, an e-commerce platform, faced challenges with digital marketing campaigns. With a monthly marketing budget of $100,000, the conversion rates were at 2%, resulting in a cost per acquisition (CPA) of $50. The goal was to improve the conversion rates and lower the CPA.

Data Analysis Approach:

1. Data Collection:

- Collected data from Google Analytics, Facebook Ads, and internal databases.

- Historical data showed that the highest conversion rates were on weekends and during specific promotional periods.

2. Exploratory Data Analysis (EDA):

- Analyzed website analytics data to identify high-traffic but low-converting pages.

- Discovered that the mobile checkout process had a higher bounce rate, affecting overall conversion.

3. A/B Testing:

- Conducted A/B testing on ad creatives and promotional offers.
- Found that a specific promotional offer resulted in a 10% increase in conversion rates.

4. Attribution Modeling:

- Employed attribution modeling to analyze the customer journey.
- Discovered that social media ads played a significant role in influencing conversions.

Outcome:

1. Optimized Marketing Budget:

- Reallocated the budget based on channel performance.
- Reduced spending on display ads (CPA: $70) and increased budget for social media ads (CPA: $40).

2. Targeted Campaigns:

- Launched targeted campaigns for mobile users with an optimized checkout process.
- Customized ad creatives to highlight the specific promotional offer that led to higher conversions.

3. Conversion Rate Improvement:

- Observed an increase in conversion rates from 2% to 3.5% after implementing changes.

- Monthly conversions increased from 2,000 to 3,500.

4. Cost Reduction:

- Lowered the CPA from $50 to $28, resulting in a 44% reduction in acquisition costs.
- Achieved a higher return on investment (ROI) with the same marketing budget.

Key Takeaways:

Through data-driven insights, XYZ Mart successfully optimized its digital marketing strategy, resulting in tangible improvements. The targeted campaigns and budget reallocation based on data analysis led to a significant increase in conversion rates and a substantial reduction in acquisition costs. The optimized checkout process for mobile users and the identification of a high-performing promotional offer showcase the practical impact of data analysis on driving successful digital marketing campaigns.

This example illustrates how businesses can leverage numerical data and specific metrics to make informed decisions, demonstrating the concrete outcomes achieved through a strategic and data-driven approach to digital marketing optimization in the e-commerce sector.

7.2.2 Analyzing Real-world Data Sets

In the realm of data analysis, the true test of proficiency lies in the ability to derive meaningful insights from real-world data sets. This section explores case studies that delve into the intricacies of analyzing diverse and complex data sets, showcasing the practical application of data analysis techniques in solving real-world challenges.

1. Healthcare Outcomes Analysis:

Objective: Understand the factors influencing patient outcomes in a healthcare setting.

Data Set: Electronic health records (EHR) containing patient demographics, medical history, treatment plans, and outcomes.

Analysis Approach:

- **Descriptive Statistics:** Utilized descriptive statistics to gain an overview of patient demographics, average length of hospital stays, and prevalent medical conditions.

- **Correlation Analysis:** Investigated correlations between specific treatments and patient outcomes.

- **Predictive Modeling:** Employed machine learning algorithms to predict patient outcomes based on various factors.

Insights and Outcomes:

- Identified correlations between certain treatment protocols and improved patient outcomes.

- Developed predictive models to assist healthcare providers in tailoring treatment plans for better results.

- Informed evidence-based decision-making to enhance overall healthcare quality.

2. Climate Change Impact Analysis:

Objective: Assess the impact of climate change on regional weather patterns and agricultural productivity.

Data Set: Historical weather data, satellite imagery, and agricultural yield records.

Analysis Approach:

- **Time Series Analysis:** Examined long-term trends in temperature, precipitation, and crop yields.

- **Geospatial Analysis:** Mapped changes in climate variables and their spatial distribution.

- **Statistical Modeling:** Developed regression models to quantify the relationship between climate variables and crop yields.

Insights and Outcomes:

- Identified shifts in weather patterns and their correlation with changes in agricultural productivity.

- Mapped regions most vulnerable to climate-related challenges.

- Provided valuable insights for policymakers to formulate climate-resilient agricultural strategies.

3. Social Media Sentiment Analysis:

Objective: Analyze sentiment trends on social media platforms related to a new product launch.

Data Set: Social media posts, comments, and interactions related to the product.

Analysis Approach:

- **Text Mining:** Applied text mining techniques to analyze the sentiment expressed in user-generated content.

- **Sentiment Classification:** Used machine learning algorithms to classify sentiments as positive, negative, or neutral.

- **Temporal Analysis:** Examined how sentiment changed over time, particularly around key product launch events.

Insights and Outcomes:

- Identified public sentiment towards the product before, during, and after the launch.

- Pinpointed specific features or aspects of the product that resonated positively or negatively with consumers.

- Informed marketing strategies and product improvements based on user feedback.

4. Urban Mobility Patterns Analysis:

Objective: Understand and optimize urban mobility patterns to alleviate traffic congestion.

Data Set: GPS data from ride-sharing services, traffic camera feeds, and public transportation records.

Analysis Approach:

- **Spatial Analysis:** Mapped traffic congestion hotspots and identified common commuter routes.

- **Predictive Modeling:** Utilized machine learning to predict peak traffic hours and congested areas.

- **Integration of Multimodal Data:** Combined data from various transportation modes to optimize route planning.

Insights and Outcomes:

- Identified peak traffic hours and suggested alternative routes for congestion relief.

- Informed urban planning strategies to enhance public transportation options.

- Contributed to the development of smart city initiatives to improve overall urban mobility.

5. Education Equity Analysis:

Objective: Examine educational equity and identify factors influencing academic achievement.

Data Set: Student demographic data, standardized test scores, socioeconomic indicators.

Analysis Approach:

- **Demographic Analysis:** Investigated disparities in academic achievement based on student demographics.

- **Correlation Analysis:** Explored correlations between socioeconomic factors and academic success.

- **Predictive Modeling:** Developed models to predict academic performance based on various indicators.

Insights and Outcomes:

- Highlighted disparities in educational outcomes based on socioeconomic factors.

- Informed targeted interventions to address equity issues in the education system.

- Supported evidence-based policy-making to promote educational inclusivity.

Key Takeaways:

These case studies illustrate the diverse applications of data analysis in real-world scenarios. From healthcare outcomes to climate change impacts, social media sentiments, urban mobility patterns, and education equity, the ability to analyze complex data sets empowers organizations and decision-makers to make informed, impactful decisions. The insights derived from these analyses contribute to evidence-based strategies, fostering innovation and addressing contemporary challenges across various domains. As the data-driven era continues to evolve, the importance of mastering data analysis techniques becomes increasingly evident for individuals and organizations striving for excellence in decision-making and problem-solving.

Certainly! Let's delve into a detailed example with specific numerical data to illustrate the analysis of a real-world data set.

Case Study: E-commerce Customer Segmentation

Objective:

An e-commerce platform, XYZMart, aimed to optimize its marketing strategies by understanding and segmenting its customer base for targeted campaigns.

Data Set:

The data set includes customer information such as purchase history, demographics, and online behavior. Here is a snapshot of the data:

Customer ID	Age	Gender	Total Purchases	Average Purchase Value	Days Since Last Purchase	Monthly Website Visits
001	32	Female	10	$50	15	200
002	45	Male	5	$80	30	150
...	...	...	...	...	...	...

Analysis Approach:

1. Customer Segmentation:

- Applied clustering algorithms (e.g., K-means) to segment customers based on purchase behavior, age, and website engagement.

- Chose three segments: "High-Value Customers," "Regular Customers," and "Potential Loyal Customers."

2. Descriptive Statistics:

- Computed average purchase values, frequency of purchases, and website engagement for each customer segment.

- Identified key characteristics of each segment.

3. Customer Lifetime Value (CLV) Analysis:

- Calculated CLV for each customer segment using historical purchase data.

- Estimated future CLV based on predicted customer behavior.

4. Marketing Campaign Personalization:

- Developed personalized marketing campaigns for each segment.

- Tailored promotions, discounts, and content based on the preferences of each segment.

Insights and Outcomes:

1. Segment Characteristics:

- **High-Value Customers (Segment 1):**
  - Average Purchase Value: $100
  - Monthly Website Visits: 300
  - Days Since Last Purchase: 10
- **Regular Customers (Segment 2):**
  - Average Purchase Value: $60
  - Monthly Website Visits: 150
  - Days Since Last Purchase: 20
- **Potential Loyal Customers (Segment 3):**
  - Average Purchase Value: $70
  - Monthly Website Visits: 200
  - Days Since Last Purchase: 15

2. CLV Analysis:

- **High-Value Customers:**

  - Historical CLV: $1,500

  - Predicted Future CLV: $2,000

- **Regular Customers:**

  - Historical CLV: $800

  - Predicted Future CLV: $1,000

- **Potential Loyal Customers:**

  - Historical CLV: $1,000

  - Predicted Future CLV: $1,200

3. Marketing Campaign Results:

- Tailored promotions for High-Value Customers resulted in a 20% increase in average purchase value.

- Personalized content for Potential Loyal Customers led to a 15% increase in website engagement.

Key Takeaways:

- By segmenting customers and understanding their characteristics, XYZMart could personalize marketing strategies, resulting in improved customer engagement and increased revenue.

- The CLV analysis provided insights into the long-term value of different customer segments, guiding resource allocation for targeted marketing efforts.

- The success of personalized campaigns showcased the practical impact of data analysis in driving effective marketing strategies and enhancing customer relationships.

This case study demonstrates how businesses can leverage real-world data sets, apply advanced analytics techniques, and derive actionable insights for informed decision-making and strategic planning.

Conclusion

- Recap of Key Concepts

As we conclude our journey through "Mastering Data Analysis: A Step-by-Step Approach," let's reflect on the key concepts and insights that have been explored throughout the book. This recap serves as a comprehensive summary of the fundamental principles, techniques, and best practices covered in each chapter, providing readers with a consolidated understanding of the essential aspects of data analysis.

Introduction:

The book commenced with an overview of its purpose, intended audience, and guidance on how to navigate its content. It laid the foundation for understanding the role of data analysis in decision-making processes and provided a roadmap for readers to follow.

Chapter 1: Getting Started with Data Analysis:

- Explored the critical role of a data analyst in decision-making.

- Outlined key responsibilities, emphasizing the importance of data in shaping decisions.

- Guided readers in setting up a conducive data environment, including the selection of tools and workspace configuration.

- Introduced different data types – numeric, categorical, and time series – setting the stage for subsequent analysis techniques.

Chapter 2: Essential Data Analysis Techniques:

- Delved into Exploratory Data Analysis (EDA) techniques, emphasizing the importance of visualization and descriptive statistics.

- Explored data cleaning and preprocessing methods, including handling missing data, outlier removal, and standardization.

- Established the statistical foundations for data analysis, covering probability distributions, hypothesis testing, and confidence intervals.

Chapter 3: Advanced Data Analysis Techniques:

- Explored regression analysis, from simple linear to logistic regression.

- Introduced machine learning concepts for data analysts, covering supervised and unsupervised learning, as well as model evaluation.

- Dived into time series analysis, encompassing decomposition and forecasting techniques.

Chapter 4: Data Governance and Ethics:

- Emphasized the importance of ensuring data quality and integrity through best practices and validation techniques.

- Addressed ethical considerations in data analysis, focusing on privacy, confidentiality, and responsible data use.

Chapter 5: Communicating Results Effectively:

- Explored data visualization best practices, guiding readers on choosing the right visualizations and design principles for effective communication.

- Discussed the creation of data dashboards, including the selection of components and interactive features.

- Introduced the art of telling compelling data stories, emphasizing narrative structure and stakeholder engagement.

Chapter 6: Advanced Analytics in Python and R:

- Provided an introduction to Python and R for data analysis, guiding readers through installation, setup, and basic data manipulation.

- Explored advanced analytical libraries, particularly Pandas for data manipulation and Scikit-learn for machine learning.

Chapter 7: Real-world Applications and Case Studies:

- Applied data analysis techniques to real-world business scenarios, including marketing analytics, financial analysis, and operations and supply chain analytics.

- Illustrated the practical application of data analysis through case studies, solving business problems and analyzing diverse data sets.

Conclusion:

- Summarized the key concepts explored throughout the book.

- Encouraged continuous learning and practical application of data analysis skills.

- Outlined steps for readers to continue their data analysis journey, including networking, staying informed, and building a portfolio.

This recap serves as a comprehensive guide, encapsulating the essential concepts presented in each chapter. As you embark on your data analysis journey, remember that mastery comes through practice, continuous learning, and the application of these principles to real-world scenarios. Happy analyzing!

- Continuing Your Data Analysis Journey

As you conclude your exploration of "Mastering Data Analysis: A Step-by-Step Approach," it's crucial to recognize that your journey in the world of data analysis is far from over. The field is dynamic, constantly evolving with new tools, techniques, and applications. This section serves as a guide for readers to continue their data analysis journey, providing insights into avenues for growth, skill enhancement, and practical application.

1. Embrace Continuous Learning:

Data analysis is a dynamic field, and staying updated with the latest advancements is essential. Engage in continuous learning through various channels such as online courses, workshops, and webinars. Platforms like Coursera, Udacity, and edX offer courses covering a spectrum of topics, from advanced statistical methods to cutting-edge machine learning algorithms.

2. Hands-on Practice:

Apply the knowledge gained from this book through hands-on practice. Work on real-world projects, participate in data analysis competitions, and contribute to open-source projects. Platforms like Kaggle provide an excellent environment for honing your skills and collaborating with data enthusiasts globally.

3. Networking and Community Engagement:

Connect with fellow data analysts, scientists, and professionals in the field. Attend meetups, conferences, and networking events to exchange ideas, learn from others' experiences, and build a supportive professional network. Online communities, such as Stack Overflow and Reddit's data science forums, offer platforms for asking questions and sharing insights.

4. Contribute to Open Source:

Consider contributing to open-source projects related to data analysis. Collaborating with the broader community not only enhances your coding skills but also provides exposure to diverse perspectives and approaches. Platforms like GitHub host a plethora of data-related projects where you can contribute and learn simultaneously.

5. Explore Specialized Areas:

Dive deeper into specialized areas within data analysis based on your interests and career goals. Whether it's natural language processing, computer vision, or big data analytics, gaining expertise in a niche area can set you apart in the competitive landscape.

6. Advanced Certifications:

Consider pursuing advanced certifications to validate your skills and enhance your credibility. Certifications from reputable organizations, such as Microsoft, Google, and SAS, can showcase your proficiency in specific tools or methodologies. Additionally, obtaining a certification in a specialized area like machine learning or data engineering can open up new opportunities.

7. Stay Informed about Industry Trends:

Regularly follow blogs, research papers, and publications to stay informed about emerging trends, tools, and best practices in data analysis. Subscribe to newsletters, join relevant online forums, and follow thought leaders on social media platforms to stay ahead in the rapidly evolving landscape.

8. Build a Professional Portfolio:

Create a portfolio showcasing your data analysis projects, highlighting the techniques and tools used, as well as the impact of your analyses. A well-curated portfolio serves as a tangible representation of your skills and can be instrumental in job applications or collaborations.

9. Mentorship and Collaboration:

Seek mentorship from experienced professionals in the field. Mentorship can provide valuable guidance, insights, and career advice. Additionally, collaborate with peers on projects or research initiatives to leverage collective knowledge and foster a collaborative learning environment.

10. Contribute to Thought Leadership:

Share your insights and experiences by contributing to thought leadership in the field. Write blogs, create tutorials, or present at conferences to establish yourself as a thought leader. Sharing your knowledge not only benefits others but also reinforces your own understanding of data analysis concepts.

Conclusion

As you embark on the journey of continuing your data analysis exploration, remember that learning is a lifelong process. The field of data analysis is vast and ever-expanding, offering myriad opportunities for growth and innovation. Embrace challenges, stay curious, and apply your skills to make meaningful contributions to the world of data.

The knowledge gained from "Mastering Data Analysis: A Step-by-Step Approach" serves as a solid foundation, and your commitment to continuous learning will propel you towards becoming a proficient and sought-after data analyst. Happy exploring and analyzing!

Appendix

- Glossary of Terms

To assist readers in navigating the terminology used throughout "Mastering Data Analysis: A Step-by-Step Approach," this glossary provides concise definitions of key terms and concepts featured in the book.

A

Analytics:

The systematic computational analysis of data or statistics, often employing mathematical and statistical methods, to uncover meaningful patterns, insights, and trends.

B

Bootstrapping:

A resampling technique that involves repeatedly sampling with replacement from the observed data to estimate the distribution of a statistic.

C

Confidence Interval:

A range of values used to estimate the uncertainty or margin of error around a point estimate of a parameter, typically expressed as a percentage.

Categorical Data:

Data that represents categories or groups and cannot be measured on a numerical scale. Examples include colors, types of animals, or survey responses.

D

Data Cleaning:

The process of identifying and correcting errors or inconsistencies in datasets, ensuring data quality and reliability.

Data Governance:

The overall management of the availability, usability, integrity, and security of data within an organization.

Data Storytelling:

The practice of using data to create a compelling narrative that communicates insights and findings to a broader audience.

E

Exploratory Data Analysis (EDA):

An approach to analyzing datasets to summarize their main characteristics, often through visualization and statistical techniques.

H

Hypothesis Testing:

A statistical method used to make inferences about a population based on a sample of data, involving the formulation and testing of hypotheses.

M

Machine Learning:

A subset of artificial intelligence that focuses on developing algorithms and models that enable computers to learn patterns from data and make predictions or decisions without explicit programming.

Multiple Linear Regression:

A statistical technique that models the relationship between multiple independent variables and a dependent variable.

N

Numeric Data:

Data that consists of numerical values and can be measured on a quantitative scale. Examples include height, weight, and temperature.

O

Outliers:

Data points that significantly deviate from the general pattern of the dataset, potentially influencing statistical analyses and interpretations.

P

Pandas:

A Python library for data manipulation and analysis, providing data structures and functions necessary for working with structured data.

Probability Distributions:

A mathematical function that describes the likelihood of obtaining different values from a random variable.

R

Regression Analysis:

A statistical method used to examine the relationship between one dependent variable and one or more independent variables.

S

Scikit-learn:

A popular Python library for machine learning, providing simple and efficient tools for data analysis and modeling.

Simple Linear Regression:

A statistical method that models the relationship between a single independent variable and a dependent variable.

Statistical Foundations:

The fundamental principles and concepts underlying statistical analysis, including probability, hypothesis testing, and confidence intervals.

T

Time Series Analysis:

A statistical technique used to analyze and interpret patterns in data collected over time, often applied to economic, financial, or environmental datasets.

Time Series Data:

Data that is collected and recorded over a series of time intervals, allowing for the analysis of trends and patterns.

U

Unsupervised Learning:

A type of machine learning where the algorithm is trained on unlabeled data, aiming to discover patterns or relationships without predefined outcomes.

V

Visualizing Data:

The process of representing data graphically through charts, graphs, or other visual elements to facilitate understanding and analysis.

Conclusion

This glossary provides a foundation for comprehending the terminology used in "Mastering Data Analysis: A Step-by-Step Approach." As you delve into the book, utilize this resource to clarify and reinforce your understanding of key concepts. Data analysis is a dynamic field, and a strong command of terminology enhances your ability to interpret, communicate, and apply analytical insights effectively.

Continue your exploration of data analysis armed with the knowledge embedded in these definitions, and feel empowered to navigate the intricacies of the field with confidence. Happy analyzing!

Thank You

As we bring "Mastering Data Analysis: A Step-by-Step Approach" to a close, I want to extend my heartfelt gratitude to you, the reader. Your decision to embark on this journey of mastering data analysis is a testament to your commitment to understanding and harnessing the power of data.

We've covered a wide spectrum of topics, from foundational concepts to advanced techniques, real-world applications, and case studies. The world of data analysis is vast and ever-evolving, and your engagement with this material reflects your dedication to staying at the forefront of this dynamic field.

Remember that mastering data analysis is not just about acquiring knowledge; it's about applying it in practical scenarios, solving real-world problems, and continuously refining your skills. Whether you're a seasoned professional or just starting, the pursuit of excellence in data analysis is a journey with endless possibilities.

As you continue your data analysis journey beyond this book, embrace new challenges, seek out diverse datasets, and stay curious. The field is rich with opportunities for innovation and discovery, and your analytical skills can make a profound impact.

Thank you for choosing "Mastering Data Analysis: A Step-by-Step Approach" as your guide. Your enthusiasm for the subject is what makes this exploration into the world of data analysis truly rewarding. May your data-driven endeavors be insightful, impactful, and filled with continuous learning.

Best wishes on your ongoing data analysis journey!

Sincerely,